Psychic Development 101

Laurie Barraco

Copyright © 2012 Laurie Barraco

All rights reserved.

ISBN-10: 0615732046
ISBN-13:9780615732046

DEDICATION

I dedicate this book to my husband Jim and my children, Jimmy and Nicole. I love and appreciate the love and support I receive from you ~ my family. I love you!

CONTENTS

	Acknowledgments	i
1	Intuition	1
2	Meet the Clairs	5
3	The Higher Self	9
4	Spiritual Ethics	15
5	Gurus and Teachers	21
6	Manifestation	25
7	Protection and Cleansing	31
8	Creating Sacred Space	43
9	Meditation	47
10	Tools of the Trade	59
11	Dreamwork	83
12	Tools of Divination	91
13	Astral Travel	109
14	Spirit Guides, Masters and Angels	113
15	Chakras	123
16	Channeling	133
17	Reincarnation	137
18	Mediumship	145
19	Psychometry	153
20	Animal Communication and Animal Totems	159

Introduction

Welcome to my first book! I have written this book with the intention that my readers will feel more comfortable about the metaphysical/psychic realm. I have included material I have used for years and years. This material was gained from many readings, sessions, classes, and teachings.

I decided to write this book for a number of reasons.

1. Because I would refer clients to at least 3 or 4 books in order to provide them with the content I feel is appropriate for beginners, intermediates, and experts.
2. I have received many requests to write a book that included the information I have shared with clients throughout the years.
3. I have to thank Connie Hughes for her persistence in encouraging me to write this book. Connie offered her assistance and did the editing. Thank you, Connie!

I encourage you to take your time with this book. Also, add your personal touch to some of the exercises. You may want to go back to certain chapters to re-do the exercises. I guarantee your results and experiences will be different each time. The more you work on your gifts, the more you will grow, and the more expanded your awareness will become.

How I Found My Niche In The World

I am gifted with the intuitive traits of my sign. I am a Pisces. Therefore, spirituality has always been intriguing to me. I did not always know which path to follow. I have been a teacher and a paralegal. I was successful financially in these fields; however, I was not fulfilled. I dabbled in meditation and classes to help me refine and expand my gifts over the years, yet I still did not pay attention to my dissatisfaction with my journey.

I decided to take myself out of my misery with my professional choices, which I finally realized weren't for me. We all have different passions and life purposes, and I kept being brought back to spirituality. It was time to listen.

It took less than a month for my first real professional gig to manifest. I was hired to run the front desk of a center in Bonita Springs, Florida and was blessed with the opportunity to see clients at the monthly Psychic Faire. Before I knew it, the store was thriving. My client base grew and grew, and within the next year I was renting a room full time. I was in heaven! I had finally found my purpose here on Earth. It was to share my unique ability to connect to a client's soul energy and relay the messages. It did come naturally, although even to this day I am still growing as an intuitive.

After a few years I was ready to take a huge leap of faith, which was to open my own center where people would be able to grow spiritually and to feel comfortable and safe during the process. I opened The Mystical Moon in 2007. I started my business in a small store with only 890 square feet of space, just to be safe. I kept eyeing the space next door, which was double the size and was a tanning salon with lots of rooms. After one year of being in business, I was able to double my space by moving next door, and to this day I am in the same location.

The Mystical Moon continues to grow on a daily basis. There are new clients coming through the door every day. More readers and healers are being utilized to help meet increased demands. My staff and I provide a good variety of services at the center. There are classes offered dealing with various topics, and many special events are scheduled at The Mystical Moon. There are also services such as readings and classes provided via telephone, video conferences, and webinars. The center provides a safe and comfortable environment for its clients. Everyone is welcome to shop in the store and to take advantage of the loving services provided here.

ACKNOWLEDGMENTS

Much love and gratitude to ~

Jodi LaMure for her friendship, love and beautiful artwork

Michelle Meleo for her assistance with the creation of this book

Connie Hughes and Crystal Childs for their editing expertise

Jim, Jimmy and Nicole for the unlimited support

My Mom, Patricia Kopercinski thank you

My Aunt, Barbara Elsey thank you

Marilyn and Charles Scott

All of my fellow friends, teachers, family and kindred spirits. There are so many of you! Too many to mention. You are forever in my heart and I thank you and love you for all of the support and guidance!

Laurie Barraco

INTUITION

We are all born with an internal GPS system, yet we don't all use or trust our own GPS system. Why is this? It may be in the past that we made mistakes after we thought we were so sure and accurate. Maybe being psychic is only for the chosen ones. Can we really know our futures and is it ok, isn't that against what God says? I am here to tell you we all have "The Gift." Not only do we all have "The Gift", it is also our birthright to use this gift. We all have the ability to hear from Source, it is our link to the other world and realms. This gift is intuition. We all have different means of how we receive the information. Some people see energy, some hear it, and some simply know it. Some people use tools such as cards, pendulums, crystals and runes to help them connect with their intuition. Some even hold an object and read the energy or vibration the object holds. This is called psychometry.

Within every session, I encourage my clients to take the time and to make the effort to develop their intuition. Why do I do this? At the end of the day, it is about your journey here on Earth - the choices you make and the actions you take. What better way to know what you really want, need, and how to use your gifts than to know yourself? Only you hold the keys to unlock the doors of manifestation and healing. Other people can help guide you, help point out where you may be missing the mark (sometimes in an unkind way) but you are the only who can evolve your own consciousness.

By developing your psychic abilities, you learn how to distinguish what is right for you and what is wrong. You learn what language your gut feeling speaks. You learn how to trust the warning signs. Sometimes we do not listen to the gut feelings or the first impulse and this is where we tend to judge ourselves for not listening to the internal feelings. From understanding a point in time when you did not listen, you can learn to recognize when these feelings or signs come up again in the future

I do receive guidance via psychic consultations once in a while. Sometimes it is really difficult to see what is going on for yourself. Someone else's opinion can be the exact thing you need to be able to move on. However, I do not go often for consultations. I have developed my own abilities to be able to trust myself for the most part. I also encourage clients to wait a certain time before scheduling another appointment. In that waiting period I prefer that clients learn to trust themselves and allow what we had discussed to manifest. Receiving psychic readings can become addicting. People do become co-dependent on what their psychic has to say. This is where the integrity of the counselor comes into play. An authentic coach, counselor or reader will tell you to wait a certain amount of time before you schedule your next session.

Everyone has experienced a blessing by trusting their own instincts. For example, you might decide to take the long way to work. You later find out that if you had gone the usual way, you would have been delayed by the traffic. By the time you are through with this book, you will be an expert at trusting your inner guidance. Learning to be comfortable with your intuition is usually where most people get stuck. They often think they are making up the messages. I often hear "I am not sure if it is my intuition or if it is me." Of course it is you. It might be your ego, which is something to work on as well. A simple guide to use is this: If the message is loving, non-judgmental and uplifting, it usually is your intuition. If the message is criticizing, competitive or any of the lower vibrational feelings or demeanor, then it is your ego. You may even ask "Is this message loving and kind and supportive or is this my negative ego flaring up?"

I would like to clarify about the lottery. I cannot count how many times I have been asked for the lottery numbers or even heard people ask, "If you are so psychic, what are the winning numbers?" I know my gift is not to be used to try to figure out the winning numbers. I have been told and shown by Spirit that my gift is to help others with messages from crossed over loved ones, to bring messages of validation for them and yes, to help myself grow and evolve. I will admit this; if I get the message to buy a scratch off ticket, I will purchase one. Am I holding out for the big one? No, but if I get the message to go purchase a ticket, I know it is probably a $25 winner. My abundance will come to me when I use my talents and abilities for the purpose of helping others in a loving way. It will continue to flow as long as I am authentic with "The Gift". I must walk my talk. If I do not, I am then stagnant in my growth. I know when I am not in alignment with my intuition. It is as if the lines of energy are capped. If we all developed our intuition and listened to the signs, we all would be spared a heck of a lot of heartache and disappointment. Lucky for you, you have this book to help you learn to listen to your inner guidance.

All of the chapters and exercises in this book have been created to help you trust your intuition and to help you create a strong spiritual foundation. Enjoy!

Affirmation: Beginning exactly at this moment, I will trust my inner guidance. I have the gift of intuition, it is my birthright. I now pay attention to synchronicities, signs, and words that come from other people as messages as well as my own inner feelings. I am becoming more intuitive/psychic by the minute.

MEET THE CLAIRS

When engaging in metaphysical conversations often you will hear someone say, "I am clairaudient or I am a clairsentient." What is all of this clair talk? The different psychic abilities are defined with the word clair in front of them. We all have one special clair with which we work. We also have the ability to develop the other clairs. I encourage my students to only work with one at a time, beginning with the one with which they are the most in tune.

Below I have broken down the different clairs for you to recognize with which one you most resonate. It is not uncommon for someone to be gifted in several of the clairs - to have multiple psychic channels of how they receive information.

The Different Psychic Gifts:

- **Clairaudient~** the ability to "hear" psychic energy, messages (voices) and sounds. Many hear their name being called. This is clairaudience. The voices don't usually make a physical sound. You may be the only one who hears the message(s). Also, some hear ringing in the ear. When this occurs I suggest asking Spirit to change the frequency so I may be able to tune in to the message.

Exercise: Sit in total silence, allowing messages to come and go. Keep a journal handy to write the messages you hear.

- **Clairvoyant** ~ the ability to "see" psychic energy, pictures, forms words written out and colors. Psychic vision looks a lot different than seeing with your physical eyes. Often it can seem as if you are fantasizing or dreaming. The pictures are usually viewed from your mind's eye. For myself, sometimes I will see a picture or even a word or name will be spelled out. Other times, it looks like a movie.

    Exercise: Close your eyes and simply allow images to formulate in your mind. Even if the images do not come easily, practicing will help develop this gift. Again, write or journal your experiences.

- **Claircognizant** ~ the ability to "know" facts, clear knowing. We all have had experiences where we just know the outcome or what to do. Some may call this instinct, I call it clear knowing.

    Exercise: Writing the outcome to future events will help you tune into this clair. Do your best to not second-guess what you are writing.

- **Clairsentient** ~ the ability to "feel" or sense psychic energy, the vibrations of a person, place or thing. Walking into a room, feeling the imprints left behind from the previous occupants is the gift of clairsentience. Many of us purchase items from second hand stores. Having a gift strong in clairsentience will help you select a purchase that will be a good energetic match for you.

    Exercise: Working with psychometry will help enhance this gift. Psychometry is the ability to tap into the energetic impressions of physical objects.

- **Clairgustant** ~ the ability to taste without physically putting an object in your mouth. We all can relate when someone mentions or presents us with a food that either we enjoy or strongly dislike. Our taste buds will salivate, or we may make a sour face. It is rare for this to be a person's strongest psychic sense.

    Exercise: In my opinion, this gift can become stronger by working on your mediumship abilities.

- **Clariscentrist** ~ the ability to smell an object or person without physically having contact or being in the same room as the person or object. This gift is similar to clairgustance.

Exercise: Working with meditation and psychic development exercises will help you hone in on this clair.

I intentionally did not focus too much on the clairs as individual categories for a reason. In my opinion, by working with the exercises throughout this book you will be able to enhance, as well as, embrace all of your clairs.

Psychic Journal

Keep a "Psychic Hit List" journal with you at all times. It is in this journal where you will document all the instances where you were "right" on hunches, feelings and random thoughts. Journaling these instances will help build your confidence around your intuition. After a while, you will have the written proof and documentation of how well you are able to interpret your own symbols, and therefore understand your own language.

THE HIGHER SELF

If you have been studying metaphysics, you have most likely encountered the term "The Higher Self". You may or may not have your own understanding of this concept. The relationship you have with your Higher Self is crucial to your existence, well-being and your journey here on Earth. Once you consciously make the connection with your Higher Self, the connection is made for the rest of your life.

Contacting and connecting with one's Higher Self is the most important stage in one's spiritual and psychic developmental path.

I keep an open dialogue throughout the day with my Higher Self. I check in frequently to see where and how I feel about my daily events as well as decisions I may have coming up or on the spot. When I refer to knowing yourself, the relationship to which I am referring is the one with your Higher Self.

The Higher Self

The Higher Self has been identified by many different names. There's the Divine Self, Inner Witness, Spirit, God, God Consciousness, Divine Knowing, Source, Energy, Allah, All That Is, Divinity, Higher Wisdom and so on.

The Higher Self is consciousness. It is the Light, the infinite consciousness connected to you, your personality.

The Higher Self is a consciousness. This is constantly changing, constantly evolving and expanding as we are on the physical plane.

Communication with your Higher Self can bring clarity about your past lives, your Akashic Record information, help you with discernment, keep your Ego in check and will always show you the truth. Every experience you encounter is relayed back to this aspect of you to be recorded in the records for understanding and wisdom.

Your Higher Self communicates with you through hunches, dreams, thoughts, meditations, channeling, emotions, and is the little, loving, guidance voice helping us through our lives.

Your Higher Self loves and understands you unconditionally; it would be silly to not use this connection to your benefit.

When

You may also bring in your Higher Self before speaking engagements, while working on an artistic project, when taking tests, during crisis, while teaching or counseling, while writing or automatic writing, or simply to learn about mysticism.

Some people report of hearing a voice that guides them in times of great need. Chances are this is the Higher Self stepping in to help out.

Creating A Filter

I highly suggest using your Higher Self as a filter, a go between, and the middleman to buffer the information, the energy and the psychic connection as you open to any type of psychic energy.

Let's be honest, all psychic information coming to you may not always be from the most loving and pure source. There are lower vibrational energies or entities in other dimensions, which may try to bring through information and energy that may not be for your highest and best good.

The Higher Self is the perfect vibrational match for you! There is no other guiding influence that could be a better match than your own Spirit. Your Higher Self wants you to succeed. It's your biggest cheerleader. As you grow, your Spirit grows and benefits as well. As your Higher Self expands so do you. Is this making sense now?

I have an agreement with my Higher Self that all information from other realms be filtered and brought through to my conscious and subconscious awareness. In this manner, I know I can trust the information, release doubt and take my ego out of the way.

The information from the Higher Self is always loving, gentle, and supportive. It does not judge or criticize or plant negative seeds. If you have any of these messages coming through this most likely is your ego coming through. If this does occur, sage, pray and clear yourself. There may be times of clarity and there may be times you might not connect to bring through clear guidance. Our vibrations go up and down on a daily basis; just like some days we have great hair days and some days not so much.

Does this mean I do not work with my guides or Angels or even the Masters? No, it does not. I do work with these beings; however, their messages are relayed to me through my Higher Self. This is also true when I work with mediumship. The deceased person relays the message to my Higher Self and then my Higher Self brings in the information. Does this change the message? No, in fact the process is so automatic, I see and feel the connection as if there is a clear pane of glass without any distortion in the process.

After you feel comfortable with your connection, you may work with sending information as well as have conversations and healing with other people's Higher Selves in the astral realm. You may facilitate unresolved issues in this fashion if one-on-one communication is non-negotiable.

Exercise To Connect To Your Higher Self

Be sure to begin this exercise when you will not be disturbed. Turn off phones, telephones etc. Keep your journal and pen nearby. Maybe have some relaxing meditation music in the background. Sage and clear the room as well as yourself. I personally like to hold a crystal, use some essential oils and I usually have some incense burning too.

- *Breathe in and out…breathing in sparkling, golden light that energizes every cell in your being. As you exhale, you will breathe out doubt, anxiety, and emotion/feeling that you know is not in harmony with you in this moment.*

- *As you continue to breathe, you will start to relax the muscles, the legs, arms. Your physical body becomes lighter and lighter with each breath. Now you will notice you are feeling lighter energetically. Lighter, yet more trusting in what you are experiencing.*

- *As you begin to integrate this weightless feeling, you are going to listen to the following statement "It is my intention to connect with my own divine source and to trust that what I receive as information is valid to me and the truth. I ask whatever information coming to me is my truth and that I speak this truth."*

- *Now focus on the heart center. Your heart is where you will go to retrieve clarity. Look within your heart. How does it look? What are the colors? How does it feel? Can you smell anything? I want you to look a little deeper. Do you see an outline of a person, a figure? I want you to move your attention to this being. This being is your Higher Self. Your Higher Self may look different that what others may have described in their visions.*

- *We are creating an agreement with your Higher Self. The agreement is this being is going to be the source and filter for all of your psychic information and messages. We know that this is a loving source, which you can trust.*

- *I encourage you to come here to find wisdom for yourself at any given time or moment. You may also come to this safe place for healing and comfort.*

- *There is a message for you here, listen quietly for it.*

- *I would like you to thank your Higher Self.*

- *It is now time to slowly come back to your body, back to the present moment.*

Journal your experience.

You may use this exercise as often as you like for clarity, answers, healing and to bring in peacefulness and tranquility.

Power Word

Another way to open up and plug in to your Higher Self is by selecting a word you do not hear frequently to be a trigger word. When spoken, this word will automatically help you turn on the faucet of energy.

- Select your power word beforehand
- Bring in your Higher Self
- State to your Higher Self, "Whenever I speak or think the word ____, I will automatically plug in and open up my intuition and connection to this vibration.
- When you are through with the session, thank your Higher Self and then close the space.

Automatic Writing

Allowing the Higher Self to communicate through simply writing without pausing to reflect or censor the material.

Tools ~ Journal and a pen/pencil

I would recommend working with the same notebook or journal.

Simply find a place where you will not be disturbed, allow the thoughts to gently come in and start writing. I do discourage people to not become attached to what is being written or worry about who will read the material.

Allow the thoughts and words to flow. The more you allow the energy to flow the less you will censor the material.

Some prefer to play soft music in the background. It is not a necessary requirement, however, music does set the mood.

Automatic writing is different than keeping a dream journal.

The Higher Self connection is a gift from the Creator to help us on our journey of life. We are all born with this loving guidance and are never left stranded throughout our lives. If it appears to be the case in your life, simply working with the tools and suggestions I have shared will help you reconnect and overcome this temporary hurdle.

Did you know?

The Higher Self or your Higher Consciousness is infinite! You can continue to connect with this vibrational plane without reaching what would be the highest level. There is no end point to consciousness, it just is. It is not solid; it is permeable and ever moving, growing and expanding. There is no end or limit to the potential for personal spiritual growth.

SPIRITUAL ETHICS

This is a necessary subject, yet one might question why I would have a chapter about ethics in a spiritual book. When it comes to spiritual work, I do this with reverence and am extremely mindful of the energy and the intentions I am bringing in and sending out. I have added this, not necessarily because I think my readers would be participating in negative behavior, but because my readers may encounter some of this questionable behavior from other "spiritual" practitioners. Hopefully, these suggestions and tips will bring a new awareness to those who are just beginning their spiritual path consciously.

Free Will

Free will is a birthright with which we are all born. We can exercise our choices. What makes life so unpredictable? Free will is the answer. We are here to make choices, to correct, to be tested, and to test others. What choice will you make? Will you challenge yourself? One of the biggest *faux pas* we make is trying to control others. This also includes when we observe someone else making what appears to be a big mistake. We try to counsel them, to discourage them, to help steer them in a different direction. We often take their decisions personally as if we may have failed them. This is difficult when we see children and loved ones head down a path we feel is harmful to them. This is where we learn about boundaries as well as other people's paths and journeys.

What are we to do when we see someone we care about heading down a dark path? We send light; we distance ourselves. We might not even be able to communicate with them because we are choosing not to witness a train wreck. We may need to take a step back when we are trying to control them. Sometimes we become too attached to someone else's outcome, thereby giving away our power in the process as well as being dependent upon another for our happiness.

How and when do we know to separate ourselves from these situations? We should separate ourselves when our interaction is stopping us from focusing and carrying on with our own lives, when we are becoming consumed with another's path. We do not always know what that soul is here to learn and what experiences they are "supposed" to have.

Karma

Karma is the result of your actions; intentions, and past life experiences all coming back to you as a boomerang. Karma does not have an identification tag. You do not always know why a certain situation is happening or even when the boomerang is coming back to you. Simply put… what you put out is what comes back. Often, clients wonder when the good karma is coming back. You may try to remain focused on your path as you continue to live with integrity. You are kind and loving to others, but you keep hitting speed bump after speed bump.

I encourage people to keep on going! What I see happening is they were almost blessed with the desired outcome, yet they gave up and gave in to negative temptation with self-defeating practices such as gossip, negative self-talk, or being self-centered. People often say, "Why bother? Nothing good ever happens." This is where you must stay focused more than ever. What you may not realize is tomorrow your wishes and dreams were about to come true.

Here is a tidbit of information ~ you cannot clear another's karma.

Only the individual can clear his or her own karma. No one can do it for you, and no one can make you do anything without your consent. I'm sorry to inform you that there are no victims here. Even difficult situations do have another possible outcome. Through challenges is where we often find the most growth. Experience is for our own soul's growth, even if it may not always make sense to our human minds. There is a Divine Order and a Divine Plan.

What do I do when I am challenged? I take a step back, breathe, meditate, and ask for others' energetic support. I also ask for the opinion of someone I respect and trust for some feedback, just in case I am overlooking something somewhere. I then continue to move through whatever challenge is at hand. I do know and understand that no matter what I am going through, there is a solution, and help is on the way. The Light never abandons us. The Light helps us, and there is always a blessing coming after the storm. What we are not always conscious of is that we often create the storm.

There are healers who claim that they can help heal or clear another person's karma. This is absolutely false! We learn through karma, and no one can prevent an event in your life. This is a falsehood; so do not fall for it. I have counseled clients who have paid others thousands of dollars to have their karma cleared. They have even paid to have their spouse or significant other's karma cleared. It simply cannot be done. You and you alone are responsible for your own experiences.

No one else can clear someone else's karma. This is something that we must do for ourselves. There are psychics and healers who say they can clear this karma from all of our lifetimes through some modality. I'm sorry, but if there is not an understanding of why something happened or why we keep repeating certain patterns, then where is the gift in learning? No one can do it for us. It's our journey and up to us to understand it. We can counsel other people, and it is up to them, to their own free will, to understand certain concepts.

Truth

We all have our own points of view as well as our unique life path experiences, which carry over into the way we perceive events and interactions with others. Our own perceived truth is a combination of our life path thus far, our experiences, our consciousness, and how we feel about certain experiences. Have you ever shared an experience with someone, yet you both recalled the same experience differently? Think about colors. Someone may say that looks red; another may say, "I think it is orange." Consider a movie you've seen. Some people enjoy it, and some do not. A personal truth is an understanding you have come to through your own experience or even a shared experience where you formulate an opinion through your own perception.

This subject is similar to the Free Will subject I discussed earlier. The same guidelines apply. People are entitled to their own opinions and/or truths. To relentlessly persuade another to come to your side is really crossing the laws of free will. We must **NEVER EVER** violate another's free will or try to impose our will on another. We often find this conflict in the area of beliefs, religion, politics, etc. My advice is that you should go within to see what YOU feel about certain areas. What is your personal truth? This is what is most important, and yes, your personal truths may change over time and with life experience.

All Is Between Us and The Light

At the beginning and end of each day, we really are only accountable to the Light as well as to ourselves. There can be no hiding, lying, embellishing, or excuses. You, yourself know when you are not being authentic and honest, as does the Light, the Creator energy. So, when you try to get away with something you know is not truly fair, just be ready for the karmic repercussions. Every action creates a reaction energetically. Why not start with the best of intentions from the beginning and save yourself the bumpy boomerang?

By taking personal responsibility and accountability, you are recognizing you are the creator of your world. The outside influences are opportunities to grow and move through some of your negative patterns. All catalysts have been placed in your life strategically to assist you with your growth.

You may respond, "What? I have done this on purpose? Put difficult people in my life?" Yes, you have. The Light as well as your soul knows what you need to grow. You attract to you people and situations for the growth of your soul. It is as simple as that, yet it may seem like a little bit of self-sabotage. This is the most efficient way for us to grow. Does this sound like a truth for you? I encourage you to decide that for yourself.

Motives and Intentions

What is the driving force behind your motives? Is it to do the best you can? Are your motives and intentions to prove others wrong or to one-up them? Intentions and motives are the energy, the fuel, or the elements that go into all manifestations. If your intentions are not pure, and for the highest and finest good, be prepared for a less than favorable turn of events.

When working with any practitioner, whether it is a psychic or healer, take time to question their motives. Is their motive to take care of the clients? Are they in this line of work to help and assist others, or are they in this field to make a quick buck, gather groupies, and be worshipped and put upon a pedestal? Obviously, motives and intentions are important in all areas of your life. Whether it is in your love life or in relationship with family members, do remember that there is no hiding from the Light and truth. You are the Light, and what you think, you manifest.

So what's the moral of the story? Be kind; be loving; be generous, but not to a fault; be honest; be fair; be patient; and most of all be the best you that you can be. You are a miracle manifested in the physical. Yes, you have room to grow. Don't we all? However, by becoming more mindful of our behavior and actions as well as motives, we in turn will have fewer regrets and a heck of a lot more celebrations and victories as well as a smoother ride on this journey.

Tip! When your buttons are being pushed think before you speak, act or react. Is this for my growth? Am I willing to accept the repercussions of my behavior from my reaction? How can I change my usual behavior to one that is filled with my new Higher Consciousness?

GURUS AND TEACHERS

My advice is for people to use discernment when studying with a teacher. Spiritual evolvement does not have to cost a small fortune. This is also true for private sessions costing a lot of money. More money does not necessarily mean that the teacher or spiritual reader/healer is better. Some people have the belief that in order to receive spiritual teachings or spiritual growth that it needs to come with financial sacrifice. I have encountered people who have gone bankrupt trying to find the God Source. To be quite honest, the most fulfillment will come from the personal growth that you receive from going within and learning from your relationships. Relationships are the number one way that we do evolve -- the relationship with self, with others, and with family members. Yes, teachers are a fabulous help, yet everyone is a teacher to us. There can be the mother figure, the father figure, family members, co-workers and love relationships.

There are some readers/spiritual counselors, who charge three, four, or five hundred dollars for a session, and it doesn't necessarily mean that their connection is better than someone who charges a lesser fee for their services. I have no control over what other people charge, but I try to make my sessions affordable for people, and this is out of humbleness and not an inflated ego. Again, I've heard people compare different readings, and to each his own. I do believe that you should not have to forego medical care, food, or paying your bills to go to a psychic. It's my choice to make sessions affordable for all, and it is my guideline to work with integrity.

Here are some questions to ask teacher/gurus. Are they humble with their gifts? They do not need to brag or tell you I can do this, this, and this to prove a point. Please stay away from those who promise you certain, absolute outcomes. There's no 100% guarantee. Do they have true concern for the client? Do they have follow-ups? Do they phone you to check on you if you're having a difficult time? Do they hold information back? If there is a holding back of information that first you have to go through this step, then you have to learn this, and then if you're worthy, they say they can help you advance to the next step which is another $100 or hundreds of dollars, **BEWARE**. Those are huge warning flags. This creates a lesser than/greater than dynamic. Everyone, I repeat, **EVERYONE**, is worthy of understanding him/herself. No matter who you are, we all have the potential to hold the same light and the same understanding, and there is no hidden wisdom.

With teachers, hopefully, their lives are in order. They're healthy. They have healthy relationships. They aren't trying to get you to talk about another reader or another healer or other teachings. They are confident in who they are. This should be a no brainer, but unfortunately there are lots of people who are giving advice who really should be taking their own advice or even going to their clients for advice. Does this teacher encourage the violation of others' free will, encourage doing magic against others, encourage tricking people, or agree to do a reading to spy on others? There is a lack of integrity if the answer is yes to any parts of the above question. Do they promise you that a lover will come back and be like putty in your hands? This shows a huge lack of integrity! If they promise you 100% accuracy, this is virtually impossible.

Free will is involved with every single aspect of our lives. We can look at the most likely outcome, provided the person is moving along the same progressive path they are on at the time of a reading. There are NO guarantees! A good counselor/a good reader will give you hope, tools that will help, and different areas to examine. Hopefully, he/she will be able to connect with your divinity and help you without any ego. The clearer the connection, the more this person has worked through his own ego, and the more he is in touch with your God Source the better this teacher/reader will be able to help you on your journey. Even just being in the company of certain people can help you to raise your vibration. Your teacher/guru should be the kind of person who can help you to raise your vibration. Choose carefully the guru/teacher you trust to help and guide you. Connect with your higher self and prayerfully ask if the person will work for your highest good.

We all come from the same source and are all worthy!

MANIFESTATION

We are spirit manifested into the physical. Our world or the world we each individually experience is a result of our environment, thoughts, words, and actions or reactions.

There are some manifestations, which are easier to obtain for us, and some are more difficult. For example, I am great at manifesting a really great love partner/spouse, yet I have difficulty setting boundaries with other types of relationships. The areas where we struggle obviously have lessons involved for us. We have opportunities to learn about ourselves during this process. There is opportunity to grow, to overcome negative beliefs or self-patterns, personality traits, and more. The list can go on and on. Many have studied the law of attraction, yet they are disappointed because their manifestations have not yet come true. These people are often confused and/or misled with the purpose of the laws of manifestation.

I kid you not… there are people who are unemployed, depressed, just getting out of terrible relationships, and they are applying the law of attraction by stating to the universe something such as, "I am expecting my millionaire new husband to come in and sweep me off of my feet." To be honest, this is most likely not going to happen. Why not? Well, in order to manifest anything, what we think and how we interact physically must be in alignment with the desired outcome. There must be a vibrational match.

The beauty of manifestation is the beautiful transformation that comes about in this journey. How people move through their uncomfortable places is where you see strength and changing behaviors. Another way of stating this is, "If you would like a different result, you must do things differently."

Within the belief systems of the law of attraction, there are a lot of rules and regulations, what words to say and not to say. I will simplify this to the best of my ability.

Intention/Prayer

Every thought, every word, is a prayer. This is a profound statement. The first time I heard this from a teacher of mine, it blew my mind. Wow, what words have I spoken over time that are now affecting my life? Not only is this profound, but it is a Universal Truth! We are creating whether we are consciously doing so or not. We are vibration and energy. Words and thoughts are energy as well. All go into the giant manifestation cauldron.

Ever hear this one ~ what we think, we become? This is also a truth, it's the same concept. If I would like to state an intention, I would only include myself never anyone else. Including someone else would be crossing free will boundaries. If someone asks for prayers, then I would state that person's name and send the healing energy. An example of this would be, "I send healing prayers and healing to Anthony Smith, born on April 1, 1977. May he be blessed with support and healing at this time in his life. Thank you."

If I would like to pray for a new love, I would say this. "I ask spirit to help me be in alignment for the companion in love that is for my highest and best good to manifest with grace, clarity, and harmony. I trust in the divine timing of this relationship. Thank you." I would not name anyone specifically to be my love interest.

Be Mindful Also To Watch Words Such As The Following:

- I am stressed out.
- I am unlucky in love.
- I am doomed.
- Of course I am not getting what I want.
- I have bad luck.
- Life is not fair.
- When will it be my turn?
- I am sick and tired.

Replace With Words Such As:

- I am blessed.
- Thank you for all I have.
- It could be worse.
- Tomorrow is another day.
- I am healthy.
- I have trust and faith in myself.
- I am love.
- I am deserving of all things good.
- I am patient.
- All is manifesting in perfect time.

Let's Make A Deal?

I would also avoid bargaining with Spirit. An example of this would be, "If I get what I want, I will never say a bad thing." Really? These are conditions that you are telling Spirit, "Give me what I want." You will manifest your desires when you take responsibility for what you are putting out into the Universe. There is no judge and jury deciding what you do get and what you do not. Your spiritual collective helps you decide, as well as the soul energies of others, together with the Creator collective. You do your part, and allow the rest to manifest.

Do you need to ask or pray every day for your desire? You do not. In fact more than once may actually prolong the outcome. Why? You are bringing doubt into the picture. You are not sure you have been heard, so you ask over and over and pray again and again requesting the same thing again and again. Even reading this repetition is annoying, yes? Well, it sounds and feels whiny. What is the energy behind whiny? The emotion? The vibration? Yes, this goes into the mix. When I say my prayers and or affirmations, I may repeat my intention. I only repeat my intention so that I am able to refocus my energy. I verbalize it with calm and evenness and trust. I see the words come out of my mouth as a stream of consciousness flowing out into the Universe.

I am sure you get the picture. These words are prayers and declarations. You will bring to you the vibrational match of your words. Now, do we sometimes get frustrated and angry? Absolutely, we do; however, don't stay in that space for too long. Find mantras or create them to help you through the unsure times as well as your impatient times.

Oftentimes, manifestations occur when we least expect them. We detach and let go; we are getting out of the way. In order for the goal to manifest, sometimes there are necessary steps which need to occur to create a foundation. I see them as necessary pieces to the puzzle for the picture to become complete. This may add to our timing in the long run. I don't know about you, but I would rather get the really sticky stuff out of the way, and then be able to fully enjoy the bliss without still having to deal with loose ends.

Many people give up just before their big break is about to occur. They did not trust the process. I see this all the time in sessions. People think their goals are not going to be reached, so they change directions. Then they must start all over. Chances are they will stop just short of their success. Keep this in mind when you are frustrated and things are not moving as quickly as you had hoped.

What About Magick? Can and Does This Really Work?

These are excellent questions! Yes, I sell candles and stones and lucky charms. These work to help remind you of your focus. The objects do hold vibration/energy; however, they are only one part of the equation.

Formula For Success

Intention + Tools (maybe crystals, candles) + Words/thoughts/prayers + Actions/physical step (this is also doing things differently) + Patience = Manifestation/goal

Are The Tools Necessary?

No, tools are not necessary. They do add a little help but are not an absolute element for your desire. All that is required is a sincere desire to be open to the gifts in everything in your world that do include problems, obstacles, and bad relationships. Behind every obstacle is a clue and gift of transformation. We just need to be willing to move through them.

What If I Did All Laurie Suggested and Still I Haven't Achieved My Goal?

We are not going to blame Laurie or anyone else. Some manifestations are not for our highest and best good, let alone for another's. Your higher guidance is the filter for all of this. If you are diverted down another path, it could be because there is a bigger and better gift waiting along another road. Let go of the "what if's" and focus on what is. The "what is" is still purposeful. There are many reasons why we did not manifest our goals. Some examples are as follows:

- We were not consciously creating from a loving space.
- The gift will show up differently down the road.
- You were ungrounded and not specific with your own desires.
- You were not in alignment vibrationally with your desire.
- You took the easy way and skipped a few steps.
- You crossed other people's free will choices.
- The intended goal or desire was not for your highest and best good, so Spirit stepped in and did you a huge favor.

The list goes on and on. These are a few examples for you to consider.

Simply put ~ if it were easy, would we grow and be able to appreciate how we transformed in the process? Remember your life is about the journey, not the destination.

We are all here to create. Now, if we created with consciousness and had the awareness that all we say and do goes into that big old manifestation pot, hmm… oh, the possibilities!

Prayer ~ I ask only for what is for my highest and best good. I trust in my higher power with my life's journey. All is perfectly manifesting in my beautiful reality.

PROTECTION AND CLEANSING

If you are human, then you have "baggage," anxieties, stress, fears, concerns, negative influences from relationships such as relatives, co-workers, etc. One of the most important practices that we can do for ourselves is to clear, cleanse, and release. We are magnetic, electric, energetic beings. We are made up of the four elements: earth, water, air, and fire. We are energy, swirling atoms, and molecules. Everything about us is energy… our bodies, thoughts, emotions. For example, we can feel when someone is worked up. The energy of that emotion is right there.

I've had it happen when I've gone into a restaurant, sat down, and felt that the people who sat there before had a fight, and the server will tell me that. It's amazing! So, we need to be more aware of what we're putting out to the universe. Our bodies, for example, are a denser form of energy than our emotions. Each is equally valuable and important. If we're around stressful people and situations, that energy tends to stay with us. Do we really need to take it with us? No! What can we do?

Prayer

I like to begin my day with a prayer of gratitude before I even get out of bed in the morning. I thank God and Spirit for all the blessings in my life. I try to envision the main parts of my day flowing smoothly and harmoniously, and I also pray for those I know who are suffering. I then close with my intention of fulfilling my soul's journey and ask to be the best me that I can be with love, integrity, truth, and compassion. It's a great way to start the day. At the end of the day I close with gratitude for the amazing day's gifts and lessons. I also release any worries, concerns, and stressors. I most certainly do not watch any negative television before I go to bed. The negativity stays in my mind and consciousness. We all need to be more aware of what we are putting ourselves in alignment with energetically. We should limit our exposure to the news. If we focus on the negative, then we tend to see the negative all around us. A lot of people say that there's only negativity around. If you want to try to focus and shift that negativity, when you see there's a difficult story on the news, you should say a prayer for those who are suffering. That might be a situation in which I'd also try to send some distance Reiki to shift the awareness.

Many people want to save the world, and I do think that one person at a time can start a domino effect to influence many others. Change begins with one person. One person is all it takes. If you set the example and the pace, chances are that people will ask what you are doing differently. Then you can share that. They get some of your energy, and they get it just by being in your energy field. As you evolve yourself, one of the most difficult things is that not everybody is on the same wavelength. It might happen that some people who are around you are negative, and your divine energy, your higher self is saying, "You know, this is not for the highest and best good of all that we're around this person so much." So, what might happen? They might become more confrontational. You start getting more anxiety, and you start seeing the perspective of the relationship in a different way. It's not a judgment against them, and it's so important that we try not to change other people. We allow them to be who they are without putting our expectations on them. That's where a lot of miscommunication happens with people.

If we expect others to behave in a certain way, they won't be able to fulfill our ideals for them. One of the best things we can do is to allow people to be on their journey, take a step back, and worry about ourselves. For a lot of people, it's a distraction to worry about others. They focus on other people so they don't have to worry about what's going on in their own world. There's no hiding from Spirit. I say this to people all the time.

In order for me to have this business, I need to have integrity with myself as well as with everything I believe in because I know energetically that I must be practicing what I tell others.

Reprogramming Mind, Body, Spirit, and Emotions

You may use this cleansing exercise at any time and any place where you are able to spend 5 minutes to center and go within. You may also record this exercise before hand or even change it up in time. Ideally, it would be good for you to be in private for this exercise, but honestly, anywhere is fine.

Center to become present in this moment. You can do this by checking in with your body, your mind, and your emotions and gauge if you are anxious, tired, etc. Pay attention to your breathing. Is it even and relaxed? As you become aware of your breathing, you will notice it becomes more regulated and even. If possible, open your hands to receive.

- *We will begin with the out breath. Breathe out stress, bringing in calm. Breathe out anxiety, bringing in patience. Breathe out fear, bringing in safety. Breathe out negative self-talk, bringing in self-confidence. Breathe out judgment, bringing in forgiveness, and breathe out envy, bringing in trust. Breathe out unhealthy relationships, bringing in loving relationships. Breathe out competiveness, breathing in balance. Breathe out blame, and bring in forgiveness. Breathe out pain, and bring in relief. Breathe out unhealthy foods, bringing in healthy foods (you may visualize these new foods coming in; trust what your intuition brings you), and breathe out unhealthy physical addictions, bringing in healthy physical activities.*

- *Continue to breathe in and out, breathing in love, joy, happiness, comfort, peace, faith, and trust. Breathe these out as well into the room, then to the building or wherever you are. Expand these intentions or qualities out to your town, the state, the country you're in, as well as to the world.*

- *When you feel complete, recharged, and fulfilled, come back to the room. Take a moment to ground and slowly come back to your body, and continue your day.*

Psychic/Energy Vampires

You schedule a coffee date with a friend you have not seen in a few months. You are pretty excited to see her. As the evening progresses you notice your energy level has significantly dropped after listening to how this friend's life has fallen apart. First you have heard about how unappreciated she is at work, and the story does not get any more optimistic in her home life. Her husband and children are ungrateful as well.

As you arrive home in your driveway, you notice how exhausted you are. Your head is pounding. You're irritable, and you feel as if your life force energy has been sucked out of you. What has happened? It appears your friend has fed off of your energy field, unknowingly of course. She, as well as most energy drainers, is not consciously aware that she is draining to be around. We all have experienced relationships and situations that leave us tired and energetically depleted.

The simplest solution might be to not interact with these people or put yourself in similar situations. This is not always an option. We may find work, shopping, dining in a restaurant, and family meals during the holidays, etc., all stressful and tiring, yet we realistically are unable to avoid these situations or people. I have a few simple solutions or suggestions that may help you keep your energy level high and protected.

1. When you leave your home envision a bubble of white light around yourself keeping all negative influences outside of your personal space (auric field).

2. Wear a protective amulet such as a bracelet, charm, crystal or sacred symbol on your body, in your pocket or in your purse to remind you to not allow yourself to emotionally interact with the drama or emotional

turmoil that is occurring.

3. When the subject turns toward drama, gossip or whining, change the subject or excuse yourself to leave the room (Example... Go to the restroom, take a moment to breathe, maybe even wash your hands to clear the energy).

4. As you feel the energy leaving your body, recite a prayer or mantra to help you redirect the energy or the pull toward them.

When all else fails, it might be time to communicate your truth to this person. Be aware they may not be receptive to what you are communicating. Do your best to be nonjudgmental, not rude or righteous. Simply state you are uncomfortable when the subject turns to drama and that you are trying to focus on the areas where you can be proactive, not reactive, in your life. What may happen is this person takes the conversation personally and gives you the cold shoulder. Trust in divine intervention, bless them and the situation, and move on with your life.

Saging

I do also believe in saging yourself, which is when we light the sage stick and we walk around to clear the energy of an environment, yourself, or other people. Use a container or heat resistant dish to catch the ashes and go around the house counterclockwise to take out the energy, the negativity, the stress, the worry, whatever is hanging in the air. This is an ancient spiritual custom/practice that's been done throughout the years and among many cultures. The sage has a wonderful vibrational property. It's been agreed upon since ancient times that this herb holds the vibration of cleansing. Therefore, if we all agree that this plant, sage, holds this vibration, then it does hold that magical frequency. Saging is a very important part of cleansing. I sage my body, car, crystals, and money. I don't do it every day, but I intuitively know when it's time to sage and clear. With saging, I do believe in saying a prayer and asking that any and all negativity be released and raised to a higher vibration. I give thanks for the lessons, gifts, and energy. I ask that it be recycled and used for the highest and best good of all. You may also use Palo Santo wood. It works as well as the sage does with a slightly different odor and frequency. Also, sage spray mist is an excellent alternative for those who are sensitive to smoke the sage or Palo Santo wood produces.

Crystals, Herbs, and Foods

Crystals, herbs, and foods also have distinct vibrational properties that can be used to cleanse. If we all agree that it's so, they take on the properties associated with them. Sometimes after a healing, I'll put my fingers without the water in the sea salt, which helps to purify and cleanse.

Cleansing A Space

- Water with salt cleanses and absorbs the intended area. Tools ~ Clear glass bowl, water, sea salt and 2 tea lights.

- Place the bowl in the center of the space you desire to cleanse.

Fill the glass bowl with water, leaving at least an inch from the top of the bowl.

- Add a teaspoon of sea salt to the water.
- Place the two tea lights in the water.
- Light the tea lights. Allow the tea lights to burn out all the way.

You may discard the tea lights in the trash (after they have cooled off).

- I suggest pouring the water outside and recycling the energy back to the earth to be transferred into new life. I would not pour the water down the drain. We would not want to put the energy the water absorbed down our drains. This possibly could lead to plumbing problems down the road.

Saging

Cleansing a space with sage is a simple and quick remedy to purify any space or object.

Tools

- Sage, either a wand or the loose bagged sage will do. It is a matter of personal preference.
- A lighter, a shell or fire/heat resistant container to hold the sage or to catch the ashes from the sage and a feather is needed.
- Although a feather is not a true necessity, it does add a nice touch to the cleansing ritual. The ashes will stain a carpet, so sage with care. It is better to sage rather than be sorry.

I open a door or window a crack to allow the negative vibrations to leave the premises. Next, I light the sage, not a lot but just enough to get the smoke going.

I walk and go to the right, going counterclockwise, to pull out the undesirable energy. I walk through each room, open closets, get up in the corners and under furniture. I continue around the entire space until I work my way back to the beginning point making a complete circle. While I am burning the sage I may repeat a prayer or mantra to help release and bring in loving vibrations.

There is a Latin Prayer that you might use ~ The *In Nomini Padre* that has been used for a very long time.

The Abbe Male Spiritus

In Nomini Patris (In the Name of The Father)

Et Fili (and the son)

Et Spiritus Sancti (and the Holy Spirit)

Abbe Male Spiritus (Be Gone Evil Spiritus)

Abbe Male Spiritus

Abbe Male Spiritus

In Nomini Patris

Et Fili Et Spiritus Sancti

In Nomini Jesu Christi (In the name of Jesus the Christ)

Amen (So be it)

If the smoke or sage burns out, relight it. You may need to do this repeatedly to keep the sage going. When you are finished with the saging process, you may tamp out the sage and save the rest for another time.

An added bonus to the cleansing process is that after the sage burning is completed, you might choose to burn Sweetgrass. Sweetgrass brings in the sweet vibrations such as the angelic, etheric realm.

Keeping Your Home Clear

There are several tips I use to help keep a space clear. I encourage you to use your own personal guidance along with the information I am providing here. There are so many stones you may substitute for these cures. These are suggestions.

1. Place 4 stones in the corners of your home and or room. Suggestions ~ Black tourmaline, pyrite, hematite, jet, selenite, black obsidian.

2. Place a mirror facing the direction where negativity is coming from to deflect negative energy. (Example - a noisy neighbor.)

3. Before painting a room, write words describing the feeling or intention you would like to infuse in your space. (Examples - love, harmony, integrity, abundance, and peace.) You may also use this method before placing carpet or tile on your floor.

4. Do your best to keep your home as clutter free as possible.

5. If you have the luxury of building your own home, you may like to strategically place clear quartz points in the foundation creating a grid for your home.

Auric Field Cleanse

Protocol

- A crystal wand of Selenite, Clear Quartz, Smokey Quartz, or Kyanite. These are just a few examples. You can do this for yourself, or a friend may help you as well. For this exercise it is best to be standing (of course, there may be exceptions where the receiver may sit or lie down).

- Start with a crystal wand placed in your left hand. Raise the crystal above the head of the receiver. Move the crystal from the top of the body down to the front of the body to the feet.

- Move a few inches to the right. Repeat the motion of moving or sweeping the crystal above the head down to the feet. Repeat this action until you have moved around the entire body. As this process is being repeated, it is best for the receiver to visualize releasing and being cleansed by the crystal.

- When finished, you may complete by spraying an elixir made from crystal essence or essential oils.

Vibrational Clearing

Cleansing yourself, as well as your personal space, may also be achieved through drumming, ringing a bell, playing a crystal or Tibetan bowl, or using the voice through a mantra or toning.

When I drum or play the crystal bowl, I do so in a controlled manner. For example, I strike the drum, wait a second or two, and repeat around the room, person, or space until I feel the energy has shifted.

An example of toning would be repeating *Ohm* for several minutes until you feel the energy shift.

The vibration created by sound resets the molecules or frequency within the immediate area.

Incense

There are many incense blends out there to help clear a space. I recommend Nag Champa, Dragon's Blood, Chandan, Frankincense, Sage, Copal, and Amber, just to name a few. These are incenses I have used in the past that have been successful in shifting the energy in my personal and business space.

We are energetic beings. Energy is constantly moving and changing. It is honestly unrealistic to think you will always be vibrating at the same frequency on a daily basis. Therefore, protecting and cleansing, hopefully, will become a daily practice.

I do feel it necessary to add here that you please do not use the intention to control anyone, even if you feel they are sending you negative energy or thoughts. We must never violate free will and project thoughts or energy to another in order to control. You may place the white light or bubble around your own body, thoughts and personal space, but leave other people out of your intention. What you may consider protection and what is right or wrong may differ from what others may see as acceptable. Trying to control or influence another will only energetically backfire on you.

Once you begin clearing your energy field, you will begin to feel a lot lighter, more optimistic, sleep more soundly, and raise your vibration.

Summary:

The tools and suggestions given in this chapter are very helpful; however, the number one way we can protect ourselves is to be conscious of our thoughts, words, and deeds. By speaking, thinking, and behaving with a higher consciousness, we vibrate at a higher frequency. Negative actions attract negative situations. Negative words reflect negative thoughts and words in your direction. If you find yourself regretting a conversation or unpleasant thought, you may ask or pray for forgiveness. Do this with the intention of trying not to repeat the offense in the future, and also with an understanding of why you behaved so. Loving words and actions most definitely attract loving conversations, loving people, and loving situations.

Did You Know? Did you know we humans have a huge effect on our weather? Where there are natural disasters, there is the need to unify and cleanse the affected geographical areas. What can we do? Be authentic, love and try not to hurt each other.

CREATING SACRED SPACE

Creating sacred space is, in my opinion, the most important, yet overlooked, step while working with psychic energy. I wouldn't dream of beginning a session with a client before creating a loving, serene, cleansed environment. Nor would I meditate, facilitate a healing session or teach a class without setting the space.

Why Do I Take The Time and Energy To Prepare With Reverence?

I have complete respect for the Light. What is the Light? The Light is one of the terms I use for the Creator, God, Soul Energy, All that Is, Allah, and the Divine, etc. I understand that the clearer the messenger and the surroundings, the clearer and stronger the connection and the ability to connect.

What If I Saged Yesterday? Is It Necessary To Go Through The Protocol Of Clearing Every Time?

The answer is yes! Energy is always flowing, never the same from moment to moment. Where we are energetically from one moment to the next is a constant movement. There are many factors to take into consideration. For example, we may have a bad day or someone is in your home or meditation room with a negative attitude. Stress, anxiety, fear and grief also affect the energy within and around us.

After saging/clearing the room, I am now ready to build the energy ~ build/create Sacred Space.

Within my Sacred Space I have already created an altar, music is playing, my intent or focus for working in this divine space.

1. As I enter in my Sacred Space I am now ready for a healing/meditation, reading etc. I envision a circle or bubble around the room or around the area I will be working. I see this bubble or protective circle around the room, under the floor or carpet and above the ceiling. This bubble serves as a deflector or energy to keep out as well as containing the building of energy I am creating.

2. I next call in the directions. (See below) Not necessary or an absolute, but a nice addition.

3. I usually say a prayer asking for guidance, clarity, protection and healing.

4. My work begins whether it is a meditation, healing, or other spiritual work. I have even created sacred space as I am writing this book.

5. Upon completion of my ceremony, class etc. I release the spiritual help/energy and open my bubble of light and protection.

Calling In The Directions

Why Call In The Directions?

Many cultures, spiritual practices and beliefs work with building 4 walls of protection, as well as acknowledging the elements. We are creating and building energy. As I have mentioned before, as we connect with teachings and beliefs from a lineage, it reinforces or connects us with those energies and vibrations.

- ***Face the East*** – *I call to the East, the element of Air, the bringer of clarity and enlightenment. I call to the Eagle to assist us and carry our prayers and intentions to new heights.*

- ***Face the South*** – *I call to the South, the element of Fire, the bringer of healing and inspiration to our lives. I call to the Wolf to help us heal our wounds and to assist us as we create our new beginnings with hopeful anticipation.*

- ***Face the West*** – *I call to the West, the element of Water, bringing in inner reflection and cleansing of our emotions. I call to the Bear for introspection and clarity with our dreamtime.*

- ***Face the North*** – *I call to the North, the element of Earth, the bringer of earthly manifestations, as well as, connection to our Ancestors/the Spirit Realm. I call to the Moose for self-esteem and confidence, bringing in self-worth and trust.*

- ***Face the Center*** ~ *I call to the Center, the element of Spirit the center of my being, my connection to my Divinity. I bring in the spark and the Light.*

As part of the opening of my circle, I acknowledge the four directions or pillars of protection. For example, I might turn counterclockwise, nod my head in each direction, say amen in each direction or simply say thank you.

Bringing in gratitude and releasing the spiritual energy is acknowledging the assistance from the spirit realm and is simply respectful. These are higher vibrational beings, reverence within any spiritual work is highly recommended.

MEDITATION

Benefits Of Meditation

- Leads to a deeper level of physical relaxation
- Decreases muscle tension
- Reduces PMS
- Helps with weight loss
- Can help cure headaches and migraines
- Improved lung function
- Enhances energy, strength and stamina
- Builds self-confidence
- Increases creativity
- Improves relationships
- Helps one cope with stress, anxiety
- Less aggressiveness
- Develops intuition
- Greater tolerance
- Brings in more patience
- Prevents wrinkles
- Helps you live in the moment
- Brings in mind, body, spirit harmony
- Connection to Higher Self/Spiritual Beings

- Increased Oneness consciousness
- Attainment of enlightenment
- Ability to see larger perspectives/Divine Order
- Meditation is Free!

The list goes on and on, these are just some of the results and benefits you may and can experience from a regular meditative practice.

You can only benefit from meditation. There is not one negative side effect.

My number one recommended remedy for almost every ailment, situation or obstacle is go meditate, go within, connect with your inner self and center your being. You can meditate anywhere, there isn't any complicated equipment and it is easy to learn. The only obstacle is not being able to quiet your mind.

What Is Meditation?

Meditation is a quieting of the mind, relaxing the body, allowing thoughts to come and go, a vehicle to connect to your God Source. A plugging in, so to speak, to your Higher Self to retrieve solutions to problems, to understand order within chaos, to send healing to another as well as ourselves, to connect with crossed over loved ones, and to communicate with Angels, Spirit Guides or Ascended Masters, just to name a few possibilities within your meditative practice.

Studies have found with regular meditation, you can reduce the levels of stress and healthcare usage, increase the longevity and quality of your life, increase intelligence and so on.

Laurie's Suggestions For A Productive Meditative Practice
Time

If possible plan to meditate at least 5-10 minutes per day and at the same time daily as well. Select a time when you are least likely to be distracted. Hopefully you will build your meditation to at least half an hour daily, up to one hour, if you are motivated to open up spiritually. Ideally, meditating in the morning as well as in the evening would be the best suggestion in order to receive optimal results with meditation. Starting your day with optimism, sending out prayers and contemplating; and ending the day with healing and releasing possible stress would pretty much guarantee a fabulous night's sleep, healthier bodies, younger-looking skin, less stress, better and happier relationships, and stronger psychic abilities. Who wouldn't want any of these "side effects"?

When Is Not The Best Time To Meditate?

After a meal, if you are extremely hungry, or while under the influence of alcohol or drugs. Even if you are sick, you can benefit from meditating. Meditation can help you repair the physical body through visualization and releasing stress, and in turn can help you move through illness.

Surroundings

I encourage you to create sacred space for your meditation. If at all possible create a meditation room for yourself, decorating and creating your own personal environment. If you do not have access to a separate room, select a room where you will not be disturbed, preferably a low traffic area. The room should be as clutter-free as possible. Televisions and electronics can cause interference with your meditation practice; not just with the noise, but with the electronic smog. If removing the electronics is not an option, I recommend placing a fluorite crystal or salt lamp near the appliance in order to neutralize the ions.

Meditating in the same room will improve your meditations. By meditating in the same place you are creating a vortex of energy, you are changing the frequency of the room. After a short while, most likely you will feel a shift gears as you enter into the room where you meditate. Others may comment on the calm, peaceful feeling when they enter your meditative sanctuary.

Tools

- Candles
- Incense
- Oils
- Crystals
- Music
- Comfortable clothing
- Bells, chimes
- Sage
- Journal, pen or pencil
- Rattle
- Sea salt
- Intention
- Headphones (optional)
- Tissues
- Tape recorder to record your messages if you prefer not to stop to write down your messages or insight
- Oracle or Tarot Cards
- An open mind and heart

These tools are suggestions, but are not necessary. The only necessary tool you would need is you.

Meditation Positions

Most teachers encourage or teach you to meditate in an upright position, however, many feel more comfortable lying down. The only drawback of meditating from a reclined position is you may fall asleep; but it is really not that big of a deal if you do. You always receive energetically on a soul level what you need or are able to handle in the present moment.

- Sitting Upright in a chair or on a cushion

- In the lotus position, legs crossed
- Lying down on a bed, on a mat or on cushions
- There are many yoga positions for meditations
- Sitting with hands open to receive
- Legs uncrossed to allow the flow of energy to circulate (except for the lotus position)
- There are also different mudra positions you can research

Breathing

There are many suggestions or beliefs on the subject of meditative breathing. All are valid and purposeful however, if you are just beginning your meditation practice I suggest keeping your techniques simple. You will know when it is time to try a new technique.

Simple counting in…one….two…three breathing out….one….two….three. Slow controlled breathing will help you focus. Counting the breaths will help your wandering mind in the moment. Simple breathing exercises are a simple and easy way to release stress.

1. The expanding balloon. This is the technique I use the most. As you breathe in, envision light, golden light coming in through the nostrils, filling your entire physical being with this healing light. As you exhale, breathe out as if you are blowing a bubble with bubble gum. This expansion represents your consciousness, awareness. As you continue to breathe you extend your focus and awareness with your Spirit, the collective consciousness, out into the cosmos, etc. After you have completed your meditation as you breathe in, see your auric field and your awareness being brought closer to your physical body, the room you're in as well as seeing yourself safely landing and grounding in your current surroundings.

2. There are various Yogic breathing techniques. I suggest if you are interested or intrigued with the Yogic breathing, research on your own to see which practice best suits your needs.

Types Of Meditation

1. **Breath Watching and Counting Meditation**
   This simple meditation technique helps you relax and wind down simply by observing your breathing. You can see the breath as cleansing coming in through the nostrils and clearing and cleansing as the breath leaves the body. Again, this is a quick and simple way to meditate and connect.

2. **The Empty Mind Meditation**
   One of the most difficult meditation techniques I have come across is emptying the mind completely, allowing thoughts and insights come in for growth and enlightenment. This is where the negative ego can run rampant. The way I work with this type of meditation is I prepare my sacred space with soft music playing (sometimes I meditate in silence) I allow my breathing to become relaxed, slowly the thoughts or insights start to flow into my consciousness. I usually keep a pen and a journal nearby in case there are some answers or insights I would like to revisit down the road.

3. **Active Meditation**
   Have you ever zoned out or received great clarity while walking, or sewing, fishing, exercising, or painting? Drumming is an excellent active meditation. The rhythm and repetitive action give your mind a job allowing the mind chatter to simmer down.
   For some people it is extremely difficult to relax or empty the mind. They allow themselves to let go, expand and receive insight while participating in an activity. If this describes you please don't feel you are a failure at meditation. As I mentioned earlier, not everyone is able to empty the mind. It is helpful to document your messages, you may forget later on.

4. **Contemplation Meditation**
   Meditating upon a question, concept or teaching, going within to receive clarity, guidance and understanding. Honestly, we all have the answers within.
   Trusting yourself is the most difficult part of any type of meditation. I suggest you select a topic, or ask the question before you go into a meditative state. Keep the pen and paper nearby to record any of your answers or messages. As you state your intention for the meditation (ex. I would like to learn about my

past lives.) You would begin with your breathing. As you breathe, see your question or speak your question out loud, then allow yourself to relax into a meditative state. You may see or feel the answers, or you may not. Try not to judge yourself throughout this process. Oftentimes the answer or understanding may come to you later as you are busy at work, cleaning your home or even in your dreams.

5. **Simple Mantra Meditation**

   Mantras and prayers have been used for centuries as a vehicle to help connect with the Divine. By simply repeating a word or a mantra, you are able to focus on your meditation in case your mind wanders. You are able to expand your consciousness while staying grounded and focused.

Mantras

- Ohm ~ the purest name of God/Creator
- Om Namah Shivay ~ Acknowledging the Higher Self, bringing in reverence, honoring your inner being. It has been said this mantras vibrates in your heart repeatedly after spoken.
- Om Mani Padme Hum ~ This chant brings you joy and peaceful vibrations. It has also been said this chant brings in abundance as well.
- Hu (pronounced Hue) ~ Opens your heart to love and transformation, can also help you move through challenges.
- Tao (pronounced Dow) ~ Means the path, the way. To learn more about Taoism research the Tao Te Ching.
- You may create your own affirmation or mantra. It may sound something like this: I am the Creator of my own experiences. Another affirmation is: I am open to the blessings of the Universe. Or, I am at Peace in this present moment.

I encourage everyone to create a safe place, haven, or sanctuary visual within his or her meditation practice. A place you can visit frequently to receive answers and clarity. You may invite your Higher Self, Guides, crossed over loved ones, Angels etc. to your Meditation Haven for answers, understanding and more. It is a meeting place created by you, you can trust your go to place for healing etc.

Before you begin this meditation, I encourage you to create your sacred space, sage, and/or play music. Find a place where you will not be disturbed for the duration of your meditation, turn off your phone, tv, light a candle, light an incense stick, play some soft music in the background, and of course, have a pen and paper/journal nearby.

Create Your Meditation Haven

- *Begin with some cleansing, deep breaths, releasing the day, becoming more relaxed and focusing upon your breath. In and out, filling your lungs with oxygen, exhaling doubt, worry, fear, letting go of what no longer serves in this moment.*

- *As you continue to breathe, your body becomes lighter almost weightless, your awareness is becoming expanded. You feel your auric field expanding and growing outside of the room, the building, you feel lighter and lighter.*

- *Now bring your awareness to your heart center. This is the center of your being. You are creating your own personal meditation sanctuary in your heart center. This is a place you can come to at anytime for clarity, truth, understanding and answers. As you focus on the heart center you may notice it appears to be a little out of focus, use your breath to see more clearly. A path appears as you look into your heart center. Take notice - is the path paved? Is it grassy, are there stones along the path? What do you see? Keep moving along this path. Take a deep breath, can you smell your surroundings? Is it warm or cool along this path, what colors do you see straight ahead? Take a look to your left, take a look to your right, look above your head, look down along the ground. I want you to observe everything your see, hear and feel along this path to your Haven.*

- *We are now approaching your Haven. Take a break before you approach your Haven. Do you see a building? Or is your Haven out in the open in nature? Are there steps? Are there trees? If you see a building take care to notice all around the building. What type of building do you see? A cabin? A beach bungalow? An apartment building? A cave?*

- *Now I'd like for you to approach this Haven. Step inside, what do you see, hear and feel inside the threshold?*

- *What colors do you see? If you are indoors, is there furniture? If not, you may now decorate your Haven with your thoughts. Create an altar in your Haven. In the future, objects may be placed there for you as keys or clues. You may also furnish your Haven with a couple of chairs or a couch or recliner for visitors such as your Angels or Guides.*

- *Take a seat and relax, you deserve this quiet time to reflect. Open up to the guidance coming through for you here in this moment. You may encounter a visitor. Know that all is well and safe in your Haven. You have taken the precautions to ensure a healthy, safe place to retreat to when you would like to meditate and connect with Spiritual energies. Take as long as you need to recharge yourself right now…*

- *It is now time to leave your Haven, you may return here as often as you wish. The more you visit this Haven the more easily you will be able to receive and connect energetically to this Meditation Haven in the etheric realm. If there were any guests thank them, bow, hug, whatever is appropriate at this time. Turn and exit your Haven.*

- *Start walking back the path to your Heart Center. Absorb the sights and impressions down this path as you had before, noticing every detail as it becomes imprinted in your memory. As you near your Heart Center you become more and more aware of your physical body, the room you are in, you will also retain the impression of all that had occurred in your Haven. Slowly move your hands, fingers, legs and neck. When you are ready, open your eyes and record your experience in your journal.*

You may record this meditation beforehand, ask a friend to guide you through or guide yourself through by memory

The best advice I can give regarding meditation is to please leave your expectations behind. Everyone's experience is unique and different. I have been in groups where one person may have a very detailed meditation describing every color, every detail with crystal clear messages. At the opposite end of the spectrum someone might feel the whole experience was a blur and they are not sure what happened or where they went. There are times when I drift off, fall asleep. There are also times when I have difficulty quieting my mind with repetitive thoughts swirling and interfering with my meditation. Don't give up!! Meditation is an important key along the path of enlightenment, soul evolution, healing and forgiveness. The path becomes more familiar and easier to access the more you travel down it. There is no such thing as an unproductive meditation. You are multidimensional, therefore it is impossible to know exactly what is going on with your entire Soul Entity. You might be downloading information in another dimension while your personality self is clueless to what is happening in the other realms. Always trust that you receive exactly what is appropriate for your Soul at any given moment.

Finally, practice, practice, practice! The more time and energy you dedicate to your meditation practice the more you will receive from your meditations. You'll be glad you did (so will the people around you!)

TOOLS OF THE TRADE

I own a metaphysical store where you may find many different crystals, herbs, candles, incense and books. These "tools" can help you enhance your intuition, bring in more protection, heal your mind, body and spirit - the uses are endless. On a daily basis, at least 3 or 4 new clients come through the door. They all have the same questions...What do I do with these crystals? Or, what are these herbs for?

I feel I do need to add a little side note here. These tools are not the magical answer to our problems. Do you need all of the tools listed below? Of course not, the intention and willingness to look within and heal what is not in harmony with your desired outcome is all that is really required. The way they can help us is by helping us focus. Simply by asking for love, you will bring to your awareness all the obstacles to work through to get to that true love. The tools do have a frequency and will help you take notice of what is missing or what may be corrected. For example, you may light a candle for a specific outcome. By divining how the wax drips and how the flame burns you may see more clearly what action may be required on your behalf.

There are thousands of tools to work with, I am sure there are many I have not worked with yet, but I am always open to new ideas.

Here are some of the personal practices I share with my clients.

Altars

Altars have been used throughout the beginning of time. Almost every religious or spiritual organization integrates an altar along with their practice of spirituality.

An altar is a representation of the Divine, All That Is, God, Spirit, Creator, whatever you call your Source of Divinity.

When creating an altar, I recommend taking the time and care to plan how it will look and what items will be placed on it. We are charging our intentions, using the altar as a focal point. The altar represents a portal to the Divine. Therefore I would not be carelessly placing objects on my altar, and I would be sure to place an altar in a sacred space that will not be disturbed or disrespected.

Where May I Create An Altar?

I recommend creating an altar in a space where it will not be handled, where it is quiet, on top of a dresser, some people create a special drawer for their altar, on a table, on the floor, outdoors, depending on the intention and facing a special direction.

East ~ new beginning, bringing in new clarity

South ~ healing, inspiration, movement

West ~ going within, retreat, dreamtime

North ~ connecting with ancestors, for manifesting earthly desires

A Typical Altar For Myself

I usually begin with my focus or intention with what I am hoping to achieve. It may be as simple as an altar in your meditation room.

Supplies:

- A table or flat surface
- Tablecloth
- 1 tealight
- A bowl for water
- Water
- An incense holder and an incense stick
- An affirmation or oracle card (for a message of the day)
- A dish with some herbs (maybe sandalwood or rose petals)
- Maybe a crystal or two

Protocol

1. Begin with saging the room where you will be creating your altar as well as saging the items you will be placing on your meditation altar.
2. Decide which direction you would like to have yours in. (East, South, West or North)
3. Place your tablecloth on the flat surface.
4. In the East direction place your "Air" element, your incense and incense holder.
5. In the South direction, a tea light or "Fire" element. You may use any candle in this area.
6. In the West direction place your "Water" element, a bowl of water or a seashell.
7. The North direction is the "Earth" element placement, place your bowl of herbs or crystals, depending on your selection of items.
8. Light the candles.
9. Pull an affirmation or oracle card (this step is optional)
10. Now it is time to charge your altar with your specific intent.

Now your altar is working, blessed, and activated. I treat my altar with respect; it has become a sacred space. I would never dream of putting any scraps or trash on it. I would also respect anyone else's altar or spiritual tools. Always ask for permission before handling anyone else's sacred tools or belongings such as a photo, a statue, a crystal etc.

Is It Necessary To Create An Elaborate Altar?

More is not necessarily better. A simple altar may contain a clean surface and a candle or simply a picture or a statue. Treating your altar with respect is the most important element, in my opinion. Remember, this is a place where you invite your Higher Self, Guides, your Ancestors, Angels, and is ideally a magnet for higher vibrational energies to come through and connect with you.

Crystals

Crystals are alive. They hold a vibration and resonate at different frequencies. I have witnessed the energetic effects of holding different crystals and watched the aura around a body change colors while that person was holding a crystal. Crystals can transmit energy, amplify, or absorb energy. Did you know that when an acupuncture needle is coated with quartz, its effect is enhanced by 10%? Even holding quartz can double your auric size.

Each crystal is unique and resonates at its own frequency. There are crystals for abundance, healing, love, protection, psychic development and more. They even come in different sizes and shapes, as well as, rough and tumbled. In the area of crystals, bigger is not necessarily better. Some stones may be purchased rough or tumbled. I encourage you to make your selection based on what resonates best with you.

Selecting Your Crystal

One universal understanding/teaching is the left side of the body receives energy, the right side sends energy. I personally integrate this practice throughout my teachings as well as for my personal usage. I encourage you to give this a try. You may find the opposite to be true for you.

There Are Several Different Methods I Use In Selecting A Crystal:

1. I research a particular property I would like the crystal used for. For example, I would like to increase the flow of abundance within the business. I refer to my crystal book, write down a list of crystals for that intention. I then go to a store and specifically go the crystal - in this case citrine. Next, I run my left hand over the crystals and see where I feel the magnetic pull, hold the crystal in my left hand. When I feel I have a match, I then purchase the crystal.

2. Another method I use is allowing my intuition to guide me. I will allow the energy of the crystals to speak to me and then select a crystal (using the same method as above with my left hand). I do trust whatever the property the crystal holds is the property required with assisting me to bring a more abundant flow within my business. There may be some blockages of which I am not aware. All crystals are purposeful. I haven't found a crystal I did not like or vice versa.

3. I have had others select a crystal for me. This method is allowing the Universe to select for your highest and best good. I have also found crystals in interesting places. To me, this is also allowing the Universe to pick for me.

4. Once in a while I will select several crystals, place them in a bag, close my eyes, and select one with my left hand. Again, this brings in opportunity for moving through blockages of which I may not have been aware.

5. Allow your personal pendulum to make your selection.

Cleansing

When Do I Cleanse My Crystals?

After purchasing, when I have completed a healing or intention, or when I feel the stone is full of energy. What if you do not clear your crystals? They may break or the energy emitting off of the crystal may feel stagnant, or they may not be able to perform your intended request.

Sage

Light the sage wand or leaf, hold the crystal or crystals over the smoke. While holding your crystal over the smoke, ask for the crystal to release and clear. Visualize white light surrounding your crystal.

Sea Salt

You will need sea salt and a bowl or a dish for this method. Fill your bowl with an inch of sea salt. Place your crystal in the sea salt, leave in the bowl for at least 3 hours. I do not use water with this cleansing ritual because some crystals do dissolve in water. The sea salt in itself will cleanse and purify your stone.

New Moon

On the evening before the New Moon place your stones outside from dusk to dawn to cleanse and clear them. The energy of the New Moon takes away energy this is an excellent time to remove old stagnant energy.

Running Water

Be sure your crystal is one which will not dissolve in water. Simply hold the crystal under running water. A few examples of running water are: a faucet, a stream or river, or under a fountain. As the water runs over the crystal, see the stone becoming purer and clearer, washing away the "old" programming and influences.

Spray Mist

Spray your crystal with a mist used for cleansing or clearing. Lemon, lavender, sage, or palo santo are just a few examples of the sprays I personally use to bless and clear my stones.

Placing On Top Of A Quartz Cluster

Place your crystal on top of a quartz cluster for at least 12 hours.

Bury In The Earth

When you feel a crystal needs to be cleansed, you can bury in a pot or directly in the Earth, leave for 12 hours, and then retrieve your refreshed crystal.

Charging

Why charge our crystals? As I mentioned earlier, crystals have an intelligence or vibration. By charging or dedicating our tools, we put our energy in them. Their vibration shifts and holds the intended purpose. It is best to give your crystal a job to do. Get to know your crystal, meditate and journal with it. Be open to any higher guidance that may come through meditation regarding this crystal.

It may take a few times to anchor the intention with your crystal. After charging your crystal, detach and proceed.

In my opinion, it is best to charge your own crystal, however; you may charge a crystal for someone else. Be sure to detach after charging the crystal especially when charging for someone else.

Getting To Know Your Crystal

After acquiring a new crystal and cleansing it, I like to spend a little meditative time with my new purchase. I sit and connect with the crystal, go into a light meditation, and I start to ask questions of it such as:

- For which purpose would you like to be used?
- How shall I use you? In a bag, by my altar, etc.

- What impressions am I feeling from this crystal? Is it warm? Tingly? Etc.

- How would you like to be charged? In the sun, moon?

- Would you like to be placed with other crystals?

- Are you to be given away when we are through?

- Are there any special messages or is there any guidance for me at this time?

(You may notice the information regarding how to work with this crystal differs than the "usual" purpose of this stone. I trust the individual messages received from the crystals.)

Full Moon

On the evening of the Full Moon is a great time to charge your stones. Simply gather your crystals and put them outside at dusk and leave them there at least until dawn. They will now hold the energy of the Full Moon. As an added bonus, you could research ahead of time to see what the energy is of the Full Moon that month and how to use it to your benefit.

I begin with a written intention of what it is I would like for the crystal to do.

Example ~I purchased a rose quartz to help heal my broken heart.

I have already formulated my intention. Sometimes I also write it down on a piece of paper.

It may go something like this ~ It is my intention for this rose quartz to help me heal my broken heart. Please help me heal completely and gently so I may move forward in a positive manner. Thank you.

After charging my crystal, I next decide how I will work with the crystal.

I Have Charged My Crystal Now What?

There are numerous ways to work with the crystals. Here are a few of my favorite usages:

In Your Hand

You may hold the crystal in your hand. In the left hand to receive and bring in the energy. The right hand will help you send out the desired energy.

On Your Body

Lying down placing crystals on the body where there may be pain or to bring in a specific energy to a chakra is always helpful. What if you would prefer to sit up? This might sound a little different, but if I prefer to sit in a meditation I will either band aid or tape a crystal to my body. I might take a small lapis lazuli and Band Aid it to my third eye to help open up my intuitive center. I have also used headbands to hold crystals in place.

I have placed crystals in my pocket, in my purse, in my wallet, in a bag in my pocket, in a bag on a string around my neck and yes, even in my bra. Placing a rose quartz close to my heart will help me feel self love or help me get through grief.

On Your Bank Account Statement

Placing a jade or citrine on your checkbook may help bring in abundance. You may even bless and clear your money. Money changes hands many times; chances are there may be a lot of negative energy on the money. By clearing your money you are also bringing Light to it and sending Light to others as well. By charging and blessing your money before you make a deposit, you are also blessing your bank account….something to think about!

Strategic Room Placement

You may intentionally set the mood for a room with crystals. For example: your child may have nightmares. Blue Lace Agate placed under a mattress will help your child sleep more soundly.

On Someone's Picture/Your Picture

Sending loving energy to someone or to yourself may be achieved via placing a crystal on a picture. Say, for example you are having some difficulty communicating with others, placing a blue stone charged specifically for healthy, clear communication as its intention on a picture of you will or may help you in the area of communication. You can use this for healing or protection, just to give a few more examples.

By The Bed

I also recommend calming, relaxing and gentle stones by your bedside if you are wishing to sleep a little more soundly and peacefully. I have lithium, charoite, amethyst, blue lace agate and lepidolite in a dish by my bed.

Under Furniture

Under my Reiki table is black tourmaline, aquamarine and rose quartz. I have pyrite under the mat by my front door for protection.

Gridding

Intentionally placing crystals in a specific layout is known as gridding. You may grid to charge food, money, an intention, or bring in a specific energy in a healing - the list goes on.

To bring in energy, I suggest using pointed crystals such as clear quartz points with the tip directed toward your intention.

We can also take away energy or clear energy. I suggest using a pointed crystal with the tip pointing away from the intention. I would take away energy when a home or room feels heavy, when taking away stress from a person, or when there may be pain or sorrow. These are just a few examples.

Example ~ I would like to activate my business bringing more life, activity and abundance.

Tools ~ Business card, a candle, 6 clear quartz points (either rough or tumbled), a jade crystal, my written intention, a lighter and sage.

1. Sage or cleanse yourself. Before working with an intention, it is best to cleanse yourself with either sage, incense, a spray, or a prayer.

2. Written intention: I am Laurie Barraco, it is my intention to bring in abundance, new clients and a healthy expansion to my business The Mystical Moon...thank you.

3. Place the business card on top of your written intention on an altar, table, or desk somewhere where the environment is calm and peaceful. Be sure you are able to check in on your intention.

4. Place your 6 clear quartz points facing the business card then place the jade in the center of your business card.

5. The candle (in a protective holder) is just above your business card.

6. Recite your intention, light the candle, focus on the flame and allow the checks to start coming in.

Keep in mind this intention is setting a chain of events in motion. Be mindful of obstacles popping up. These obstacles are opportunities to work through your abundance issues. Happy manifesting!!!

In Plants

You may place a few moss agates in with your plants to enhance their growth and keep them healthy.

On Your Food

I have placed crystals on top of my food as well as on top of medicine (through the container or box) to enhance the nutritional benefits.

What To Do When They Are Done With You?

You may bury, give away or place it back into nature. Sometimes they make themselves disappear. In some cases they break for no apparent reason, either the stone has served its purpose with you or it may have needed to be cleansed. My favorite stone is a piece of moldavite. I have "lost" this stone on several occasions. Somehow it manages to come back to me. I try not to question, I trust in the Light it holds and its purpose with me.

Crystal Essence Sprays

I love using crystal sprays. You may create an ambiance in your meditation room, healing room or even business.

Simple Recipe

Tools ~ Distilled water, spray bottle, rubbing alcohol (to help preserve the blend) and a crystal.

1. Fill your bottle with distilled water almost to the top.

2. Place your crystal in the bottle.

3. Add 5 or 6 drops of the rubbing alcohol into the bottle.

4. While holding the bottle in your hands, envision the blend becoming activated by your intention.

5. Place in the sunlight with the cap on for at least 12 hrs.

6. Enjoy

Please research the properties of every crystal before you begin any type of work with them. There are several which can be toxic.

Suggested Must Have Crystals For Your Spiritual Toolbox

These are a few of my favorite crystals to work with. I have also listed a few qualities these crystals possess.

Clear Quartz~ Clear quartz can be used to help enhance other crystals. They are energizers and amplifiers of energy and thought. It enhances psychic ability and helps with memory. It also brings in calm and harmony and aligns the chakras and the circulatory system.

Rose Quartz~ Stone of great love, friendship, romantic love, self-love and mothering love. It helps heal emotional wounding and pain and helps heal the physical heart. It may also help with fertility, as well as, with the grief of miscarriage.

Amethyst~ Helps open the crown chakra connection to the Divine Self. It assists with addictions, psychic ability, psychic attack, and alleviates sadness and grief. Eases headaches, pain and swelling.

Infinite~ The most powerful and effective physical healer I have come across. Stimulates physical, emotional, spiritual and mental healing. Good for betrayal and grief. Connects us to the angelic realm.

Lapis Lazuli~ A stone of truth and friendship. There is a very strong Egyptian connection. Use for meditation, communication and protection.

Black Tourmaline~ Helps absorb negativity, stress and anxiety by deflecting the energy and creating a healthy circuit. Excellent for grounding and focusing.

Kyanite~ Wonderful for meditation, aligning the chakras and never needs cleansings. It releases anger and frustration and helps with the throat chakra. It is also a natural pain reliever.

Scolicite~ Beautiful loving heart energy. Peaceful, meditative, pure, creates a heart-to-heart connection when used in relationships. It is excellent for dream recall.

Amber~ Used for teething for babies. Protective and healing. Helps release disease and activates the healing process. It has a strong feminine Goddess connection.

Fluorite~ Has been used to alleviate electronic smog. I have fluorite next to my computer to help neutralize the negative ions. It deflects psychic attack and negativity being sent your way. It opens up intuition, focus and energizes the body. It is very good for the joints.

Pietersite~ Is said to contain the Keys to the Kingdom of Heaven. It activates the third eye, meditation, metabolism and helps recognize truths.

Angelite~ Great for astral travel, the throat chakra, inner guidance and faith. Heals throat, thyroid and circulatory systems. Connects us with our Spirit Guides, Angels and crossed over loved ones.

Carnelian~ The Artist's Stone, it unlocks creativity and inspiration. It helps with shyness. It also prevents nightmares and brings in personal power. It is great for increasing libido.

Prehnite~ Brings in Archangel Raphael for healing. The healing stone for healers. Energizes the body, calms, and is excellent for meditation. It is helpful for healing kidneys, gout and anemia.

Laboradite~ Brings in self-confidence, enthusiasm and harmony. It enhances intuition, and a deeper knowledge of the Mysteries. Heals with eye disorders and metabolism.

Hematite~ Improves relationships and helps one move through grief. Deflects negativity, brings in protection and is best if worn on the left hand. It is good for the intestines and blood flow.

Citrine~ Wonderful stone for the solar plexus. Brings in abundance. Put in your cash register.

Oils

I use essential oils for meditation, divining, relaxing, healing applications, sanitizing, blessing, anointing, in a diffuser to clear and cleanse a room, and those are just a few of the ways that I use the oils.

How They Work

There are certain fragrances/aromas that will resonate with you and of course there are those which will make you scrunch up your nose. I encourage you to research the fragrances which are unpleasant to you to see if there is an area you may be struggling with. Some scents will trigger memories from past lives, they may be familiar, bring in anxiety, or be calming and invigorating.

Guidelines

Before using any essential oil, please make sure you thoroughly read the labels and do your own investigation to be sure of the quality and if there are any topical warnings. Some oils are of a lower synthetic quality and some people are extremely sensitive to different blends or oils.

Topical Applications

Crown of the head, forehead, temples, behind ears, neck, upper and lower back, hands, feet, reflexology points, ankles, over vital organs. When I apply the oils on my body, I usually pour a couple of drops into my hand, breathe, then apply to the other area or areas to which I feel drawn to apply.

Usages

1. If you are experiencing a headache, you may use a blend of oils specifically for relieving headaches. Put a drop or two on your temples and in the palm of your hand. While inhaling, envision the pressure and discomfort of your headache gently lifting.

2. You can use oils to anoint people, candles, an intention etc.

3. Add rose, hibiscus, ylang ylang, peppermint or jasmine in your bathwater for a relaxing and calming bath.

4. You may wear a pendant with a chamber and put some oil on a cottonball, and wear around your neck or hang it in your car.

5. A few drops on a cottonball, placed either in your vacuum bag or with your a/c filter becomes an air freshener.

6. Place a few drops of lavender in a bowl of water next to your bed for a pleasant night's sleep.

7. Oil diffusers freshen up a room as well. You can find oil diffusers just about anywhere.

8. With medical supervision, you can help improve organ function and more.

9. During a meditation to enhance, relax, or open up your intuitive connection.

Creating Your Own Oils

You can create your own personal oils. Grapeseed, almond, jojoba, sunflower or coconut are good for the carrier or base oil. It is best to use the amber or blue bottles to keep them fresh. I have blended a few of my own single oils to create a specific blend for myself, my family and clients with much success.

Recommended Oils

Lavender ~ healing, calming, nurturing, heals skin ailments, helps with restful sleep.

Peppermint ~ energizing, mental clarity, digestion, stomach issues, headaches.

Clary Sage ~ mellow, warm, helps calm hormones, wonderful for women.

Lemon ~ uplifting, sanitizing, relaxing, mental clarity, purifying.

Frankincense ~ skin issues, meditation, and protection, found in many creams.

Patchouli ~ helps with negative emotions, meditative, helps with nausea.

Eucalyptus ~ loosens up tense muscles, good for allergies, sinuses and breathing problems, used in mouth rinses.

Orange ~ brings in joy, inner child healing, opens the heart.

Candles

I love using candles. I use them in almost every aspect of my work. I use them for healing, meditation, psychic connection, protection, when I am teaching, and for divining.

They light the way, burn away negativity, cleanse the spirit and help me build momentum with my intended manifestations.

Candles are wonderfully versatile; you can add oils, herbs, select different colors depending on your intention, write a specific message on them, the possibilities are endless.

Colors

Red~ Passion, Physical Love, Family Matters, Root Chakra

Blue~ Communication, The Moon, Peace, Channeling, Throat Chakra

Green~ Healing, Abundance, Heart Chakra

Black~ Protection, Absorption of Negativity, Root Chakra

White~ Protection, purity, peace, connecting to Spirit, Crown Chakra

Pink~ Self-Love, Romance, Heart Chakra

Purple~ Intuition, Spiritual growth, 3rd Eye Chakra

Brown~ Grounding, Physical Property, Pet Healing, Root Chakra

Orange~ Strength, Success, Healing for Intimacy, Creativity, Sacral Chakra

Yellow~ Communication, Cheerfulness, Assisting with Willpower, Solar Plexus Chakra

Gold~ Wealth, The Sun, Royalty

Silver~ Inner Growth, Beauty Art

Example~ I would like to develop my psychic abilities, especially my psychic vision.

1. Gather supplies: purple candle, a candle holder, your written intention, a blue yarrow blend oil, some psychic-enhancing herbs (ex. dandelion), a toothpick or pencil, a journal and paper or pen to document your manifestation magic.

2. Write your intention ~ I, Laurie Barraco, am at this very moment opening my third eye so I may see more clearly psychically. So be it, so it is ~ Amen

3. Prepare your candle by dressing and blessing it. (see Dressing and Blessing)

4. Light the candle, take note of time, light your candle.

5. Allow the candle to burn for at least two hours at each lighting.

Dressing and Blessing Candles

A simple way of creating a custom-personalized candle is by dressing and blessing your candle according to your desired intent in the present moment.

Supplies

1. Intention
2. Candle ~ if possible work a corresponding color to match your intention
3. Toothpick, pencil or inscribing tool
4. Herbs
5. Oil
6. Parchment paper
7. Candle holder
8. Match

New Job

1. Begin by gathering your supplies and having a paper towel or cleaning supplies nearby ~ Sometimes blessing and dressing can get a little messy.

2. Written Intention ~ I, Laurie Barraco, born March 12th, 1968 have as my intention to manifest a new job that will provide a safe, professional and abundant environment for my career path. So be it, so it is, Namaste'.

3. Write your intention on an orange candle (in this case) holding the candle on its side and going around the entire candle with my inscribing tool (toothpick, pencil etc.)

4. For this particular purpose, use Come to Me Oil. Place a few drops on your finger and apply the oil around the entire candle (except for the wick).

5. Next take your mixed herbal blend and roll the candle in the herbs. The oil helps the herbs act as an adhesive to collect the herbs.

6. Place your candle in the candle holder, place the candle holder on top of your intention, light your candle, and allow the flow of events to occur in the future.

Be sure to take the necessary precautions whenever working with fire!

I might journal as I observe the burning candle ~ allow the candle to do its magic.

Herbs

Herbs are unique and vibrate at different frequencies just like the crystals. Herbs can and may be added to oils, incense, food, candles and more…

Lavender~ Soothing, healing, protective and nurturing.

Peppermint~ Mental clarity and focus, good for stomach aches and lifting your mood.

Hibiscus~ New creations, sexuality, love and warmth.

Red Sandalwood~ Calming, good for meditation, and mental clarity.

Red Rose Buds~ Enhances prophetic dreams, healing, love, luck and creativity.

Frankincense~ Uplifts spirits, helps remove negativity.

Copal~ Used in spiritual rituals for purification, spiritual connection and cleansing.

Jasmine~ Abundance, love, sweetness of life.

Clove~ Divination, aphrodisiac, love, peace of mind, and psychic development.

Blessed Thistle~ Financial, spiritual and physical blessings.

Patchouli~ Love, money, prosperity and fertility.

Uses

1. Candles ~ You can make candles with herbs in the wax. I like to "dress" my candles with oil and roll them in herbs. I am able to create special custom blends with this method.
2. Bath Blends
3. A little mojo bag
4. Incense Mixture
5. Blends for protection
6. In the 4 corners of your home
7. Around the perimeter of your home
8. You may cook with intention. (Ex. Whip up some muffins with herbs and ingredients which resonate to the vibration of healing. Lavender muffins are very soothing, calming and tasty!)

Please research any herbs that you are planning to consume to make sure they are safe for consumption.

Incense

Incense is another tool I use frequently and is another use for the herbs. I usually burn incense sticks. There are many single herbal incenses, as well as, blends. You may refer to the properties of the herbs listed above and burn accordingly with your desired intention.

Some of my favorite incenses are: The Blue Nag Champa, Dragon's Blood, Chandan, Moldavite, Lavender, Frankincense and Myrrh, Patchouli, and Spirit Guide. Most metaphysical stores will carry these popular blends.

You can also create your own incense blends with the herbs.

Tools

- Herb
- Mortar and pestle
- Charcoal
- Heat resistant container (ex. mini cauldron)
- Sand or dirt to buffer the heat

I plan ahead with my intention of the desired energy or ambiance I'd like to create.

For a protective and cleansing blend, I use copal, sage and rosemary.

1. Sage yourself before any type of energetic work.
2. Place the copal, sage, and rosemary in the mortar and blend the herbs with the pestle.
3. Place the incense charcoal in the heat-resistant container and light.
4. Sprinkle the herbal mixture over the charcoal, envisioning cleansing and clearing.
5. Allow the herbal mixture to cleanse and clear.

Do your research. There are certain herbs which are toxic and should never be burned indoors

Also remember to watch your fire

Bath Salts

Bath salts are easy and fun to create. I like to use sea salt to blend a few herbs (of course ones that I know are safe for my skin), blend an essential oil and voila! Instant healing bath mixture.

Laurie's Love Yourself Bath Blend

Supplies~ A large bowl, Red Rose Petals, Lavender, Sea Salt, Jasmine Oil and Orange Oil.

- Mix all together, allow to marinate for at least 24 hours.
- Recite this Mantra~ I love myself completely and unconditionally.
- I am a beauty internally and externally.
- I am love.
- I am light and I am worthy.

Laurie Barraco

DREAMWORK

Dream interpretation has been called a special gift and an art form, but the truth is, anyone can interpret their own dreams successfully. Many people claim they do not dream; however, everyone dreams. The simple fact is that we do not remember our dreams all the time. Learning your own dream language can bring you healing, clarity, and an understanding of who you are and what your journey here on Earth is about. Pretty profound, yes? Our dreams are the gateway to our souls, our Higher Selves, and the sub-consciousness without our ego in the way. The best part of dream work is that we do not need extensive training or degrees. A little effort, discipline, and the willingness to do the physical, mental, emotional and spiritual work in your life can and will bring you closer to your personal fulfillment through your own dreams.

Dreamwork

I have worked with healing; sending light with the intention of healing and repairing relationships, and memories by sending a request before I go to sleep to heal or possibly work through some issues or struggles I may have in my life at the present time. I have used my dreams as a guideline to see where I am at in my life professionally, health-wise, psychically, in my personal relationships and to see where my hidden fears, anxieties and stressors may be rooted.

How Do I Get Started?

You may begin your dreamwork at any time. There are a few suggestions, tools and tips I personally work with in my own dreamwork with which I have had successful results.

Tools

Dreamwork does not require a lot of tools or preparation. However, there are a few suggestions I do have to help enhance your experience. These will assist you with relaxation, sleeping more peacefully, as well as, help you condition yourself in remembering your dreams:

- A journal to help record your dreams. Almost a requirement in dreamwork. You will need to be able to record your dreams. We all have had experiences where we thought we would remember our dream, only to later have forgotten the key details.
- A pen or pencil to document your dreams.
- A tape recorder is an excellent alternative to writing down your dreams. The benefits of taping your dreams are: minimal effort is required and you won't have to deal with messy, unreadable handwriting.

Some Extra Dream-Enhancing Tools Are:
- Calming, soothing essential oils either on your bed sheets, your pajamas or on your body such as lavender, chamomile, rose or some custom blends created to enhance the dream state such as Young Living's Dreamcatcher.
- Crystals which promote sleep and dream recall, such as rose quartz, blue lace agate, amethyst, moonstone, selenite and lepidolite, just to name a few.
- Soft music before bed. I listen to either a crystal bowl or a soft music cd with headphones before I go off to sleep.
- Drinking soothing tea before bed (without caffeine) will help you sleep.

- Reciting a prayer or mantra can help with conditioning before bed.
- Read a spiritual book. Books I read before bed: Jane Roberts, Jacqueline T. Snyder, The Zohar (anything from the Kabbalah Centre). I choose books of higher vibration to help me enhance my dream recall.

Sleep Preparation

In my opinion, preparing yourself is the most important part of dreamwork. The activities and mindset are crucial before we go off to sleep. One way to view the activity of sleeping is: as you go off to sleep your soul leaves your physical body. A small portion of your soul stays to keep the body alive. The rest of your soul merges with your Divine Spark, your Spirit, you are connecting with higher vibrational planes IF you prepare yourself in a lovingly, conscientious manner. This means prayer, releasing the day, setting the intention for peaceful, loving interaction in the dream state and maybe journaling or using essential oils; I am sure you get the picture. All of these actions contribute to raising your vibration. We want to raise our vibrations and it is quite simple to achieve this.

Going to sleep grumpy, angry, stressed, drunk, or under the influence of drugs are activities that are not raising your vibration, they are actually lowering your frequency. Which entry level do you think you will be connecting with in the dream state? The answer is lower vibrational planes because this is where you are. Something to think about more consciously, don't you think? You may see now where some of your nightmares come from.

I realize some people are on medication to sleep and for emotional stress. I do encourage anyone on these medications to consult their doctor before taking themselves off of any medication. The side effects of taking yourself off of any medications without a doctor's consent can be disastrous both emotionally and physically.

The Room

The condition of the room in which you are sleeping also affects your dreams and the messages you receive in that state. A room filled with clutter does not promote a healthy flow of energy or Chi (life force energy).

Simple Suggestions

- Keep the room you sleep in as clutter-free as possible.
- Sage frequently, or use sage spray. Palo Santo will work well too.
- Limit the amount of electronic appliances in the room. Electricity can disturb your sleep.
- If someone is a snorer, use earplugs.
- A dreamcatcher in your room does help keep the room clear of negativity.
- An electric salt lamp is a great ionic cleanser to help remove the negative ions.
- A bowl of water with a dash of sea salt by the bedside can absorb negative thoughts (ex. stress).
- I would not suggest lighting a candle before bed. You may drift off to sleep before you extinguish the candle.

Remembering Your Dreams

The most common statement I hear is "I do not dream" or "I can't remember my dreams". The first suggestion I have is to change your words and thoughts to "I do dream" and "I am able to remember my dreams clearly".

Remembering your dreams is and can be as simple as changing your previous program. Stating before you go to sleep "I will remember my dreams that contain information that are for my highest and best good." Will you remember all of your dreams or even remember a dream every night? Most likely not. Some dreams are recalled later in time and some aren't meant to be remembered at all. Please do trust your Higher Self is working with you for your highest and best good. Some dreams might actually complicate your mind and bring your dreamwork to a screeching halt.

Types Of Dreams

There are many categories of dreams. Below are a few different categories of dreams. Although some dreams you may not be able to define, you may need to analyze them if you are encountering a closed door.

- **Fear or Stress Dreams** ~ these dreams show us where we have most of our anxieties. Sometimes we do not realize how subconsciously we have a deep-seated fear. If you have these types of dreams do not worry, they are normal. You can bless, surrender, and ask for opportunities to move through and heal these fears and anxieties. For some, counseling might be the best course of action. Many of us who are in relationships have negative dreams about our partners and then we wake up angry. These dreams are messages of where our possible fears are and maybe where we have not completely forgiven. Your partner may or may not get a chuckle out of these dreams. My advice? Surrender and ask for more assistance with your healing process.
- **Premonition Dreams** ~ you dream of future events. Some premonition dreams come true and manifest, others may not. Now, we all have free will and there is no direct one solution to all of life's situations. Many people believe a certain event will happen because they dreamed it, but this is not necessarily a fact. As I mentioned, there is free will of all parties involved in all scenarios. Just because you dreamed it does not mean it will happen. This is where a dream journal can come in handy so that down the road you can see how your prophetic dreams manifest. You may also experience a few Déjà vu episodes. Déjà vu is travelling ahead in time and checking out possible scenarios. They are a validation that you have created and chosen this scenario.
- **Warnings** ~ you may dream about possible scenarios where it may be best to keep your guard up around certain people or situations. Again, there is free will involved; however, there may be signs or signals you may not be able to pick up on when you are awake and interacting.
- **Visits From Crossed Over Loved Ones** ~ often these dreams seem so real. Most newly departed souls visit their loved ones after they transition. Not everyone will remember the visit from their loved one, but they do usually visit to let their loved ones know they are okay and made it to the Light. Often the departed loved ones bring in messages or insights. Please do not discredit these

messages or visits. They are purposeful.

- **Negative Habit Dreams** ~ often show us where we are neglecting or stopping the progression of our souls. These dreams may contain negative thoughts, stressors, foods, people, and environments that are self-sabotaging us.
- **Confrontation Dreams** ~ we may dream about a situation with a person where we are able to speak our peace or they may be able to speak theirs. You may or may not be aware of this person's true feelings. Do you need to confront them in your conscious awake state? I do not believe this is necessary unless you have a strong inclination to speak up or if the dream was extremely disturbing. Please do use your discernment.
- **Healing Dreams** ~ you can most certainly heal relationships when communicating with another is out of the question. Before going off to sleep ask to heal the situation in the dream state with conscious understanding of what transpired in the dream. You may or may not remember your dream, always trust you will recall the information that is for your highest and best good.
- **Spiritual Dreams** ~ dreams of understanding, clarity, wisdom, epiphanies. In these dreams you may dream you were in a classroom or there was a group being led by a teacher. These dreams help us see how we are always growing and evolving. I love these dreams. I set intentions before I go to sleep of understanding some of the scenarios in my life. I ask for higher guidance, wisdom and full awareness of these situations as well as the concepts of life and purpose.
- **Nonsense Dreams** ~ these are the dreams where we have no idea what happened, who these people are, and a bunch of random symbols and messages. The dream state is the time to put into files or organize your events.

Akashic Records

A vibrational plane exists called the Akashic Records. This is where all the events of our lives, everyone else's thoughts, feelings and experiences are recorded in a depository of knowledge. Anyone can have access to this wisdom. In dreamtime we often visit this plane as well as record our events of the previous day. You may receive guidance or understanding of your past lives and memories by tapping into this dimension.

Personal Symbols

There are many dream interpretation and symbols books out in the stores. Here is the simple truth, you dream in symbols that you will understand. We all have our own dream language. You may ask others what their take or interpretation is, but ultimately it is what you take from the dream itself which counts and matters the most. Yes, there will be some dreams which baffle you, receiving anther's opinion may help you, but what you take away is what counts.

When a certain symbol keeps reoccurring ask yourself, "What does this mean to me?" Even when dreaming of someone ask, "What does this person represent to me? Do I respect them? Do I trust them? What type of personality do they have?"

Sometimes we dream of someone dying. Does this mean they are passing soon? No, not necessarily, it may mean they are going through a lot of transition at this time. They might also be encountering the death of a job or relationship.

I could include several general interpretations, but I would rather you discover and do your own personal symbol work yourself.

I will include one example: a key shows up on the ground for you. I might interpret this as the key or the piece I was looking for has shown or will show up on my path. I might even ask the question after I woke up, where was I going in my dream? What color was the key? Etc.

Gifts From Spirit

A gift from Spirit is when you dream about a certain object, song, or person, only to later encounter this object, person etc. in your conscious awake state. This is a gift of validation to trust your experience. Some people have this experience from their meditation experiences as well. If you find the blue box that you dreamed about, I encourage you to do your best to acquire this object and place it on your altar or special place as a reminder of how you are so much more than this physical body.

Where Do I Go From Here?

Begin with your dream journal, a pen or pencil, your intention to remember your dreams, and patience.

Take your time as you delve into the dream world. There will be periods of time where your dreams are profound and there will be times when you cannot recall a single dream. Be patient. The clarity, healing and personal growth is invaluable. Most of all, enjoy and have fun as you delve into your subconscious.

TOOLS OF DIVINATION

Here are some of the Tools of Divination with which I have worked. I have provided simple and easy-to-follow directions as well as some suggestions for those who are ready to dabble and experiment with some new metaphysical tools.

There are many methods of divination. There are Runes, I Ching, playing cards, and more. I am only sharing information about a few different methods or tools that I have worked with personally.

When working with any method of divination, I highly suggest a few guidelines to follow. I go over these guidelines in every psychic development class I teach.

1. Whenever working with Psychic Energy, always show respect. Respect the process, honor the messages, and do not manipulate the tool or message.
2. Only participate when in a balanced frame of mind. This means no alcohol or drugs. If you are in a bad mood, depressed, or not centered in a loving space, I would suggest coming back at a later time and date when you are more balanced and of clear mind.
3. Be specific with your questions. If you leave your questions too open-ended, you will receive vague answers.
    - Example - Am I going to move? Instead, I would ask, "Am I going to move from this current residence within the next 6 months?"

- Example - Am I ever going to be happy? A better way of asking would be, "What can I do to bring more happiness into my life?"
4. Use all divination methods with the utmost integrity, honesty, and for only the highest and best good for all.
5. Be sure to open and close with a prayer when the session is complete.

Tarot Cards

I love using the Tarot cards during my sessions. They bring a validation of what my guidance is "showing" me during my sessions. I have been teaching how to read the tarot cards for quite a few years. I have simplified the teaching of the tarot into 2 classes. The first class covers the basics, the second class goes over the spreads. I also answer the questions that may have come up in the time from the first class. There is no short cut to becoming an expert with reading the cards. There is a lot of time and practice required.

The traditional tarot has been used for thousands of years. It is the most widely-used method of divination. There are many methods and philosophies regarding how and when to use the tarot.

I always ask these questions in the beginning of the class

- Why do you want to work with this ancient tool of divination?
- What are your intentions?
- Are you willing to put in the time and energy necessary to become comfortable and confident with your cards?

Hopefully, the answer is yes, and the reason why you are working with the tarot is to grow, learn about yourself, and to tap into the psychic realms for the highest and best good of all.

There are a few guidelines I suggest if you are interested in working with cards or any form of divination.

- Only seek knowledge you have permission to seek.
- Never use this or any psychic method to find out the dirt on anyone else without his or her permission. No psychic spying!

- Treat your deck with respect and love.
- Respect the answer you receive and move on.
- Realize that sometimes you may not be of clear mind and are unable to make a clear connection.
- Always open and close with a prayer of gratitude and humility.
- If someone is refusing to be read or if you want to prove a point, it might be time for you to put your cards away and reflect on your motives.

Understand that the cards are never wrong; your interpretation may be off. The clarity in a session depends upon your ability to step to the side and allow Spirit work through you. This takes patience and practice. Give yourself time to work with the cards and your intuition.

With Which Deck Should You Start?

I suggest to people that they begin with the Rider-Waite Deck. As you study with the traditional deck, you will understand the language and symbolism of the cards. You can always switch to another deck after you are familiar with the general interpretations.

Card Care

Treat your cards with respect, cleansing them often. Cleansing can be done with sage, placing a crystal on top, or by simply asking your guides to clear them. Store them in a peaceful, safe environment in a cloth or box. I personally keep my cards on my table in my personal office with a crystal on top. There is the belief you should not purchase your own cards. I personally believe this is not a necessity. I have purchased many of my own decks and have used them successfully in my sessions.

After obtaining your cards, I suggest you cleanse them with sage, crystals, or by leaving them in the moonlight under a full moon. A great way to bond with them is to select one card a day. After selecting the card of the day, look at it. What is it telling you? Close your eyes. Hold the card to your heart to feel what the message is. What is standing out in the card? Write down your interpretation. After making your interpretation, look up the meaning. You will be surprised at how your interpretation was pretty close to what the reference book had to say about the card.

Atmosphere

It is extremely important to create a calm and peaceful atmosphere when communicating with the spirit realm. Candles, incense, and soft music are great elements to create the ambiance for working with your tarot cards. You would want to set up space where you will not be interrupted. I always set the space with a prayer before clients arrive and ask to be open to receive the messages for the highest and best good for all. I ask to help the person coming to see me to the best of my abilities.

Protocol

I always say a prayer to connect both the client and myself. This prayer also opens the door to my higher guidance. I use a simple prayer which may vary at times, but the intention stays the same.

I call upon ___'s higher self, the person's guides, and guardians. I call upon the highest and finest light that works with and loves the person to work through me with love, clarity, wisdom, hope, and truth.

The reading then takes place, and I allow the information to flow through without trying to interpret it. This does take practice. It is a complete matter of non-filtering information, not an easy task to master.

Through much practice and time I am able to connect to the Soul energy of the client. I often call my readings Soul Readings. We are here to evolve the Soul. Why not connect with the energy and listen to what it is saying? What is missing? What is on target? Why is this person here on Earth?

To Allow Others To Touch The Cards Or Not?

There are many thoughts regarding this question. I believe it is a personal preference. I allow my clients to touch and select the cards. It is up to what the reader finds comfortable.

I read for many clients over the phone from cities and countries throughout the world. It does not make a difference if someone is in front of me or not. Soul energy is soul energy. It crosses all dimensions and realities. If a client is not present in the room, I select the cards for them.

After saying the prayer, I have the client select the cards by fanning them out. You may also pull from the top. Some readers have the clients cut the cards in three piles. It is all a matter of personal preference. What the reader feels most comfortable with is what is important.

I then start with the Celtic spread and take the reading from there.

I always finish my session with a prayer of gratitude, and the session is then complete.

The Cards

There are 78 cards in the tarot deck. The first 22 cards are the Major Arcana. They relate to major life karmic lessons. The deck begins with the Fool. The story tells of his soul's journey through life. Each card has a specific meaning. The cards have corresponding numbers and elements; even the colors are significant.

Reversed Cards

There are some readers who do not read the reversed cards. I do because I feel it brings in more insight; it is a personal preference. The reversed position is the opposite of the upright. Reversed is not always a "bad thing."

The next 56 cards are the Minor Arcana. They compliment the

Major Arcana in bringing more details in a reading. I see the Major Arcana as the nouns and the Minor Arcana as the adjectives to the nouns. The Minor Arcana still are significant; do not get me wrong. If there are a lot of Majors popping up, it simply means you are working through a lot of karma.

The Suits

Pentacles - earthly matters, physical, material, tangible, the physical body, money, home, career

Cups - emotions, love, relationships, water element.

Swords - air, the mind, thoughts, the thinking part of the brain, intelligence

Wands - fire, inspiration, spirituality, intuition, soul growth

Court Cards

Kings - power, achievement, responsibility, authority

Queens - feminine side, nurturing, gentle, soft, caring, positive, creativity

Knights - movement, growth, some experience (ex. - College student, courageous)

Pages - novice (ex. - Middle school, undeveloped aspect of the questioner's personality), brings news; pay attention to the next card

Numbers

Aces - new beginnings, opportunities, new cycle

Twos - partnership, relationships, communication

Threes - mind, body, spirit, creativity, temporary situations

Fours – organization; earthly grounding of mind, body, spirit; grounded; reliable

Fives - cards of difficulty, they motivate us to get out of a stagnant situation, time to move because of discomfort

Sixes - peace, harmony, family oriented, events that turn out better than expected, inner and outer peace

Sevens - wisdom through experience, very spiritual number, intuition, the search for something more

Eights - overcoming obstacles, success, change is coming, lots of forward movement, learning new skills

Nines - number of self-accomplishment, success with effort, independence

Tens - completion, end of a cycle, fulfillment, perfection of endings

As you can see, there is quite a bit of information here with the tarot. By building upon the information I have provided, you are able to have a pretty good foundation with your intuition, as well as, the simplified guide I have created here.

Some Simple Spreads

Remember these readings are based on where the questioner's consciousness is at this moment. Are readings 100% accurate? Absolutely not, there is free will which is involved. Also, there are times you are not to know the outcome, the great mystery of life. Why would we have come here if we knew all the answers? We are here to grow, change, and make decisions based on the events/catalysts in our lives.

The One-Week Prediction

You will be making predictions for the next 7 days. Start with Sunday; write your predictions for what you intuit will happen for that day. Continue on with your predictions for the next 6 days. At the end of each day, record in different ink what actually happened on that day. You will again be able to review your symbolism. This exercise is to be taken lightly, no self-judgment please. This is a simple exercise to have fun and play with your predicting abilities.

Timeline

I use the timeline to look at the possible future events. I pull 6 cards usually. You can look at days, weeks or months. I do not look into the future for more than a year's time. More than that is not as accurate. There are a lot of variables which can take place in that time.

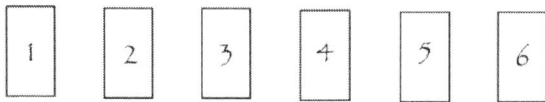

d/w/m   d/w/m   d/w/m   d/w/m   d/w/m   d/w/m

Decide whether you are using day, week or month

Quick Assessment

I use this simple pulling of 3 cards to tell the story of what is going on at the present moment.

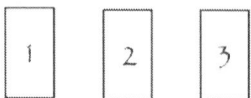

Relationships

This easy spread is used to see what the possible outcome of 2 different people/situations together for combined energy. This spread can be used for relationships, job scenarios, a choice, and more. 9 cards are to be selected.

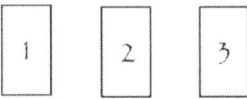

The first person/situation

The other person/situation

Combined result

Yes or No

These are pretty simple and easy to use. You would select 3 cards. You would use the reversed cards for this spread.

Up   Up   Up = Yes

| Up | Up | Reversed = Yes |

| Reversed | Reversed | Reversed = No |

| Reversed | Up | Reversed = No |

The majority of up or reversed is how you know if the answer is "yes" or "no.

Laurie's Celtic Spread

99.9% of all of my readings start with the Celtic spread. It is a great way to achieve an overall view of what is happening with the client.

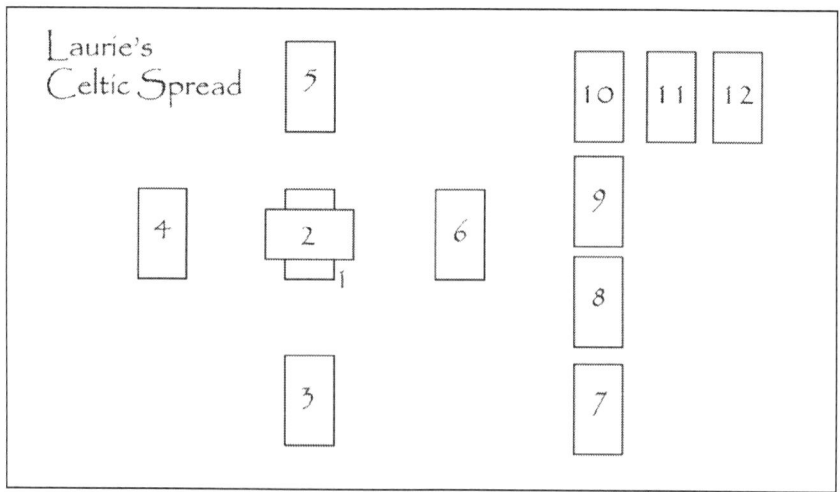

1 ~ You

2 ~ What crosses or concerns you

3 ~ Your foundation, where you are solid

4 ~ Recent past 3 months

5 ~ Message from Spirit

6 ~ Near future 3 months

7 ~ You are conscious of this

8 ~ Your environment/influences around you

9 ~ Your hopes/fears

10, 11, 12 ~ The final outcome

I encourage people to start slow and easy and then build up to a Celtic spread.

Oracle Cards

Oracle cards are cards that do not relate to the tarot correspondences. There are thousands and thousands of oracle cards. They all have the author/artist's interpretations and messages. They usually have a theme to go along with the deck. There are cards with all different messengers and themes. There are cards with angels, animals, goddesses, saints, positive affirmations, chakras, and more.

The same guidelines as the tarot cards apply when working with the oracle cards. I often have people work with the oracle cards in addition to the tarot cards. For example I have them to do a simple layout with the tarot, document the results, and then do the same layout with the oracle cards. Almost every time the message and result are the same. This is the beauty of working with divination tools. Most of the time you will receive the same answer/message.

Pendulums

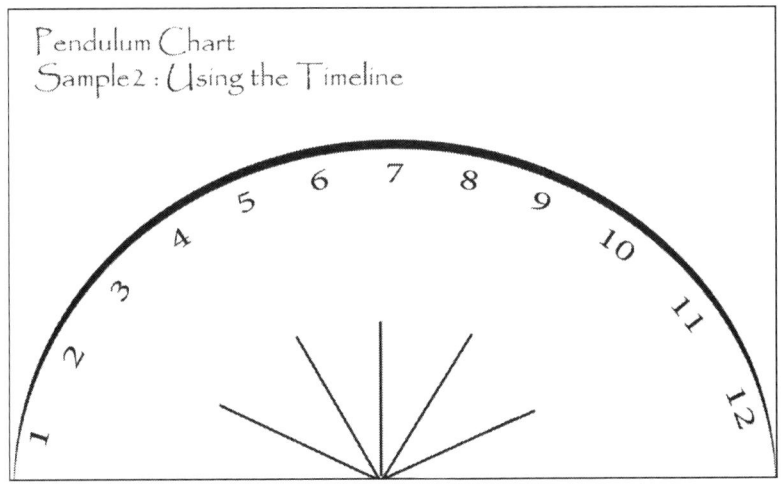

A pendulum is a tool that is used to access your Higher Self for guidance/clarity as well as answers to questions you may have. I have used a pendulum to learn which foods are good for me, to find an answer to a yes or no question, to see if my chakras are balanced, to scan body parts for imbalances, as well as for channeling or clearing a room. There are countless uses for pendulums. These are just a few examples of situations where you would be able to use the pendulum.

Pendulums are easy to make, or you may purchase one from a metaphysical/new age store. When purchasing your own pendulum, it is best to test and see with which pendulum you connect. It might move automatically when you come near it, or you might even hear it call to you.

I suggest that you hold the pendulum in one hand and place the other hand underneath the pendulum. Ask the pendulum, "Please show me my *Yes*." Then ask, "Please show me my *No*." If you do not know what your *yes* or *no* looks like, then you would ask the pendulum. A *yes* can go back and forth, up and down, or even clockwise and counterclockwise. Take note after you request to be shown your *yes*. Next ask to be shown your *no*. It should move in another direction. Very rarely will your *yes* or *no* change.

After purchasing the pendulum, you should cleanse it with sage, a prayer, or by simply putting it in sea salt without water. After you connect with your pendulum, I highly suggest you be the only "user" of the pendulum to keep only your energy on this item.

Prayer

You might want to use the following prayer to connect with your guidance (Higher Self):

I request all information/guidance/answers come from my divine source. I clear myself of all outside influences and trust the answers are being channeled via my divine guidance.

When receiving an answer, trust the answer. Please do not keep asking the same questions more than once. When you don't trust the answer, it brings doubt into your work with the pendulum.

Do realize there will be times when you are unable to receive a clear answer. Move onto another question, or it may be time to put your pendulum aside. There is always the risk of using your pendulum too much and becoming dependent upon it. Please use your pendulum with caution and discernment.

You can create your own pendulum. I have used necklaces with a crystal on the chain as well as any type of pendant on a chain. You may also use a piece of thread with a needle or even a ring on a string.

It does help to have questions prepared ahead of time. Also, be specific with questions. Be prepared to ask several questions in order to receive clear information regarding the area in question. Be sure to allow the pendulum to fully stop all movement before moving on to the next question.

Examples Of Good Questions To Ask Your Pendulum:

Am I going to move within the next 5 months? Would it be beneficial for me to move from my current residence within the next 5 months?

An Example Of A Less Favorable Question:

Am I going to move? Try to avoid being too general with your questions. You will receive better information with more specific questions.

Tips:

1. Be sure you are in a clear frame of mind, relaxed, and emotionally and physically grounded. If there is a strong emotional attachment to the subject area in question, you may not receive clear and accurate information.

2. Keep a notebook handy to write down your questions and your pendulum's response as well as names and dates for documentation.

3. Clear your pendulum often with sage, prayer, or sea salt.

4. Have only your energy on the pendulum.

You may wish to consider the following topics for pendulum consultations: Career, Love, Relationships (family, love, friends, and coworkers), Money, Investments, Physical Body, Lost Items, Foods, Sex of a Baby, Spiritual Guides, Timeline, Geographical Areas, and Travel. When I am through working with the pendulum, I close with a prayer of gratitude such as the following:

I thank my Higher Self/Higher Guidance for the assistance today. Thank you. Amen

I store my pendulum in either a bag or on top of a crystal. There are many people who carry their pendulums with them wherever they go.

This is a personal choice. If a pendulum should break, the energy might still be available for you. Only you will be able to tell if the pendulum still "feels" the same.

Tasseography ~ Tea Leaf Reading

Tea leaves have been used for divination since medieval times. People used tea leaves, coffee grinds, and wine sediments. This method involves really using your imagination. If you have a hard time trusting yourself with images, you will struggle a little with this method.

Supplies – light colored teacup and saucer, loose tea leaves, water.

- Make a cup of tea. It is best to use a light colored teacup. You also would want to use loose tea leaves.

- Steep the tea and relax the mind. A couple of minutes are all that are needed for this step.

- Sip, drink the tea, and take your time.

- Swirl the cup three times; gently turn the cup over onto the saucer. The liquid and leaves will be ready to be read on the saucer. Take a few deep breaths to center yourself.

- Take a look at the pictures and symbols. Write them down. This is all personal interpretation. If your cup has a handle, begin reading from 12 o'clock. Break up the cup into three parts - rim, middle, and base. The rim is above the tea level where you poured the tea, the middle is between rim and bottom, and the base is where the tea level was before you dumped it. Sometimes there is a circle around the cup.

- Pull it all together with your imagination, symbols, and intuition.

You can purchase a symbol or divination glossary to help you with the meanings. For example - you see an apple. An apple can mean achievement. If bubbles are floating on the top, this means money is coming. Is a glossary necessary? It is not required, but it can help you. I have participated in tea leaf readings where there wasn't a glossary handy, and the reading was very successful.

Obviously, the more you practice, the better and more confident you will become. With tea leaf readings, part of the mystique is the preparation of drinking the tea. Tea leaf readings are a lot of fun as long as you allow your imagination to flow.

Using any tool of divination is and can be of assistance to help with guidance, clarity and deeper insight. There is a fine line of abusing the methods. I have witnessed many people become codependent on the advice of a psychic. When this occurs, I wean my clients and encourage they find the solutions on their own. Readings are to help empower them and not to answer and solve all of their problems. I recommend clients not come back for another session for at least a month. Emergencies happen, but I usually encourage them to solve their dilemmas on their own. If we try to fix or solve all of their problems, we are doing a huge disservice to them. This is where our own discernment must come into play.

Tip: Remember, these are tools and aids to help you connect to psychic information. The most profound and accurate tool is your own intuition.

ASTRAL TRAVEL

Astral travel is a lot more common than people realize. We all leave our bodies during the night. Just enough soul essence is left connected to the body to keep the body alive and functioning.

You Might Have Astral Traveled If…

- You had dreams of flying.
- You visit a new place for the first time, yet it is familiar.
- You meet with someone for the first time and they are familiar.
- You share a dream with someone and they had the same experience.
- You were able to view your body from the ceiling.
- You have déjà vu (déjà vu is when you travel ahead in time, check out the scenarios to select the outcome that suits your soul's path).

These are just a few signs or experiences people have reported with astral travel.

Astral traveling is leaving the body to explore different realms for ~

- Learning experience

- Meeting with a teacher, ascended master, or guide
- To travel into the future to research different probabilities
- To visit with deceased loved ones
- Information about upcoming prophecies
- Exploring different areas of the world or universe
- Visiting a past experience to learn from the experience for deeper clarity and understanding
- Viewing past lives
- Healing
- A scheduled astral travel date with another like-minded spiritual buddy

The astral realm is infinite. In order to cover all of the dimensions and planes I would need to start another book. What I will share is how to facilitate safe and productive astral travel.

Tools

- Sage
- Candles
- An intention
- A journal, pen or tape recorder
- Sacred space (preparing the space)
- A timer
- Crystals (optional)
- Incense (optional)
- Music (optional)

Here is a sample of how I prepare for a session of astral travel for myself ~

- First I make sure I am in a relaxed, calm state of mind and my emotions are balanced.
- I always make sure I do not try to meditate or astral travel on a full stomach. This can lead to a sluggish feeling and can be difficult for lift off.
- I create my intention (ex. It is my intention to travel to Egypt to see the pyramids of Giza) I might also write this down.

- I have already decided which music I will play, the candle I will burn, and the incense I will burn. I usually select a few crystals to hold in my hand or in the room anchoring protection as well as safe astral travel.
- I always bring my guides and protection with me when I meditate, astral travel or do any spiritual work.
- I prefer to sit up when I meditate with my back straight supported by the chair or wall. At home, I prefer to do my spiritual work in my pappasan chair.
- I begin my prayer/intention and slowly go into my meditation for safe astral travel.
- Sometimes I tape myself beforehand, and then play the meditation back to guide me along my journey. Also, in the past I have recruited a friend to read the meditation/journey out loud for me. And there are times when I breathe and guide myself along my journey with my guides leading the way to my destination, whether it be to the pyramids in Giza or to a spiritual classroom for a lesson on the Akashic Records.
- After my meditation/journey is complete I always thank the assistance/protection etc. I then journal my experience.

If you expect profound experiences each time, then you are setting yourself up for disappointment. Each journey will be different. It is really hard to recreate the same experience each time. Your mood changes, your body changes, and the astrological cycles and moon cycles make a difference as well.

A successful astral travel session can be measured in this way; Did you relax? Do you have at least a slight shift in consciousness? Did you receive clarity? An answer? Did you meet someone? Are you unable to remember? This is ok too if you were able to at least quiet the mind. Repeat after me "Any time spent in a relaxed, meditative state is time well spent." You can repeat this over and over and the message is still the same ~ meditation/astral travel/quiet time is the number one way to retrieve answers, clarity and to really become closer to enlightenment.

Expanding Energy/Astral Travel

Tools ~ Optional; you may have a friend select several items to place in a box, bag or an envelope.

- Set the space with your sage, candles, incense, crystals etc. Set your intention to safely travel outside your body to "see" what items are in the box, bag etc.
- Find a comfortable place where you are able to sit or lie down (not so comfortable to where you fall asleep)

Relax

- *Take some cleansing breaths in and out. As you continue to breathe see yourself expand a little more each time. After a few cleansing breaths, bring your attention to the area above your head, the crown chakra. See your light body travel outside the top of your head and floating to the desired object, eventually traveling and looking inside to view what is there.*

- *After you feel confident of what you have viewed inside the box/container, travel back into your body through the crown.*

- *See your expandedness slowly coming back to the physical body.*

- *Continue your breathing, slowly coming back to the room.*

Journal your experience. Document colors, sensations, impressions, everything. There are no wrong answers.

Remember to use your integrity with this exercise. I strongly discourage anyone to use their psychic abilities to spy on anyone.

SPIRIT GUIDES, MASTERS AND ANGELS

Spirit Guides

Spirit guides are non-physical helpers. Many children view them as imaginary friends. They have an agreement to help us fulfill soul contracts we created before we were born. They bring in guidance, support, as well as protection, and they are a link to the spiritual dimensions. Our spirit guides do have other "jobs" besides assisting us. As we evolve, they evolve as well. They are not waiting around to jump in to save us. They are able to assist when we call to them. They also keep a watchful eye on us as they continue to do their own spiritual work. Guides may be guiding more than one person at a time. It may be hard for us to comprehend this concept because we are trying to understand or grasp this information with our limited human perspective.

Most people have at least 4 or 5 regular guides working with them at any given time in their lives. Do the guides change? Not really, your main helpers are with you throughout your life. Some of a person's crossed over loved ones become spirit guides after they leave their bodies. However, not all crossed over loved ones become guides.

Are all spirit guides more evolved? This is not necessarily so. Just because an entity does not have physical form does not automatically mean they are of equal or higher vibration.

You may have had past life experience with your spirit guides, and you may reincarnate with them in future lives. You may have also been their guides as well. This is a pretty interesting concept, right? Most of us have been spirit guides to others in between lives.

Spirit guides have names. The names aren't important to them, but a name can help you to identify them. Knowing names for spirit guides is more for our comfort. They may give us a name to call them or maybe not. I have connected with a few guides in sessions where I was unable to pronounce the name. They gave me another name or nickname to use for them.

Different Types Of Guides

- **Master** ~ your master guide is your main guide. The master guide is the one who is closest to you. If we were to look at your guides as a hierarchy, this would be the one at the top of the tier. The master is loving, compassionate, helpful with necessary healing, and is completely in service to your path. This guide usually does not guide many at once. Some people actually have more than one master guide; this is according to your path in this lifetime.
- **Joy** ~ joy guides help us lighten our hearts when we are sad, depressed, lonely, or simply stagnant. Laughter and joy raise our vibration. Being lighthearted assists with creativity and helps us to move out of stagnant, redundant situations.
- **Teacher** ~ teacher guides show us the lessons and do their best to help us move through repetitive patterns. We may attract more teacher guides as we evolve. They help us understand more about ourselves in areas of love, money, relationships, and career choices. Each experience in our lives is an opportunity to overcome, grow, and evolve. Teacher guides help us become more aware when we are missing the mark.
- **Helpers/Runners** ~ Helpers assist with specific tasks or jobs. For example if I am working on a one-time project, my helper guide might help me with the skills needed for this one project. Runners assist with finding the perfect parking space, the best outfit, etc. You can send your runners out ahead of you to help clear the path.

For example you might ask, "Could I have all green lights, please, because I am running late."

Spirit Guide Meditation

- *Sit straight up in your chair with feet flat on the floor. You may wish to say a prayer or state your intentions now. In whatever way feels comfortable to you, express gratitude, a sincere intent to work with your teacher, a prayer to God, and a request for safety in your travels.*

- *When you are ready, take a deep cleansing breath and envision a golden white light coming down upon your crown. Watch as the light moves through you slowly, going down through the head, throat, into the torso, down the arms, and out your fingertips. As the light comes out of your fingertips, it encircles the outer parameters of your body. The light proceeds down through your legs and into the floor. Imagine this beautiful light pushing out all negative energy from your body. You're cleansed, refreshed, and safe.*

- *Take a couple of deep breaths to relax, pushing away any tension or anxiety on the exhale.*

- *Envision yourself walking down a path. Pay attention to what you see. Without straining just relax and look about. What do you notice as you casually stroll slowly down the trail? Notice the colors, shapes, objects, and textres you see.*

- *Continue to breathe slowly while walking at a comfortable relaxed pace, enjoying the stroll and letting the images come to you gently.*

- *Listen to the breeze, to the calling birds, to whatever sounds are here. What can you hear as you stroll along?*

- *Take a deep breath in.*

- *What do you smell as the breeze blows? Do you smell the trees, the flowers? What is here that you can see, hear, and smell?*

- *Keep walking, slowly strolling, and enjoying the walk down this path.*

- *Feel the weather; feel the clothes on your body; feel what is around you. Notice the temperature.*

- *Continue to stroll along. Look to your right. What is there? Take a deep breath. Look to your left. What do you notice? Breathe slowly, nice and relaxed. Look above you. Take in all the sights, sounds, scents, and feelings as you continue to stroll along.*

- *In the distance you see a small home. This is a nice, cozy home. It is very inviting. Pay attention to what it looks like as you walk towards it. Continue to walk toward the house, taking in all that you perceive.*

- *You are now in front of the house. Walk up to the stoop or porch, but don't enter yet. You are about to meet your Guardian Spirit, your guide who is your highest teacher, who has been with you from the beginning. He/She is ready to meet you and to start learning how to communicate with you. You are very loved and accepted in this place.*

- *Take another deep breath, and on the exhale release any built up anxiety, making sure you feel as relaxed as possible. When you are ready, step up to the door of the house. Put your hand on the door. Notice what it feels like, notice the temperature.*

- *Take a deep breath, and open the door. There is a table and two chairs. Focus only on the empty chair, and take yourself to it. Sit down in the chair, and look up. The person sitting before you is your Guardian Spirit. What do you see?*

- *If you are overwhelmed at first, it is okay. Your Guardian Spirit knows your intentions and will wait for you. When you are ready, you may speak to him/her or simply sit and be in the Spirit's presence.*

- *When you are finished communicating with your Guardian Spirit, express your gratitude. Gently rise, and push your chair in. Turn to the door and walk out of the house. Make your way back slowly.*

- *Know that the first time you do this it may be very overwhelming emotionally. Don't let that deter you. This is your inner sanctuary. It will become stronger in time, and there is so much that you can learn here at your sanctuary.*

Your guides will leave you many different signs or calling cards. They welcome you to continue to communicate, pray, and invite them to assist in your life. I encourage clients to ask for validation of the name being accurate or at least close, or even a sign such as a feather to be manifest in the most unusual or unique places and times. For example, I was able to connect with a client's guide. The guide's name was Running Yellow Feather. Within the next week she found yellow feathers or yellow feather references everywhere. They will do this for us, and remember this is for us, not for them. They are not attached with believing in the spiritual realm. They understand and empathize with our desires for physical validation.

I personally kept a list of my guides in my journal. As I was slowly introduced to them in meditation, they each revealed a name and a symbol to me. Over the course of a few months each guide's name and sign showed up in my life. It was an extremely enlightening and fun time for me. I wrote down the signs as they manifested in my journal. I invite you to do the same. There is nothing like the validations when they start coming in.

Angels

Angels are different from our guides in that they have not lived on Earth. They are messengers, healers, and protectors and assist with just about every area of our lives. They help us restore faith, trust, and love. Angels have inspired writers, artists, musicians, as well as prophets, poets, leaders, and basically all of humanity. Many people have reported miracles where they avoided an accident, or a mysterious stranger who helped them while they were in danger and suddenly vanished into thin air.

They are a different frequency, and we must invite them in to help us with our lives. They follow the do-not-violate humans' free will code unless there is a situation where the person is going down a path which is not for the highest and best good of that soul entity. They are ready to jump into action to the best of their abilities. They appear to us as light, orbs, colors, temporarily as humans, or even beings of light with wings.

You May Have Been Touched By an Angel If You Have Experienced

- The scent of flowers
- Ringing in the ear(s)
- Soft Breezes
- Feathers appearing in interesting places
- Hearing the sound of bells or chimes
- Feeling the flutter around your head
- A flash of light
- Goosebumps on the body
- Sometimes they reveal themselves through crystals

There are different orders of Angels such as the Seraphim, Cherubim, Thrones, Dominions, Virtues, Powers, Principalities, Archangels and Angels. You can always research to learn about the different triads of angels.

Crystals To Help Connect With The Angelic Realm

- Celestite
- Angelite
- Hiddenite
- Iolite
- Amethyst
- Rose Quartz
- Petalite ~ The Angel Stone
- Lapis Lazuli

Angels and Days Of The Week

- Sunday ~ Michael
- Monday ~ Gabriel
- Tuesday ~ Camael
- Wednesday ~ Raphael
- Thursday ~ Zadkiel
- Friday ~ Hagiel
- Saturday ~ Cassiel

Assistance

If you are like me, you enjoy being specific with your spiritual helpers. Here is a short list of the archangels and some of their specialties.

- Michael ~ protection, electronics, fights darkness and protects humans in the area of service. Use frankincense and myrrh to contact him.
- Raphael ~ is the healer; he helps the healers and those in need of healing. Use anise and lavender to contact him.

- Gabriel ~ helps with children, childbirth, is the soul's keeper or protector. He assists with creativity ~ writing, music, poetry. Use jasmine to call him in.
- Uriel ~ helps us connect with our ancestors, brings in peace and justice. He also assists with weather changes. Use chamomile and sandalwood to contact Uriel.
- Metatron ~ is the mediator between the angelic realm and humans. He helps us become more motivated. Use benzoin and patchouli to bring Metatron in your life.
- Haniel ~ brings in natural healing and beauty in our lives. Use citrus aromas to connect with Haniel like orange or lemon.

There are hundreds of Angel oracle cards/decks available for purchase. I recommend Doreen Virtue's Cards. They are easy and full of information. Here are a few suggestions I have to help you connect with the angels through oracle cards.

- Select a card a day for your daily message
- Select a card to help you see what your obstacle may be
- Select a card with a specific angel before bed put the card either under your pillow or next to your bed. Ask the angel to bring a message through during your dreamtime.
- Select a card before making a decision

4 Directions With The Angels

Select 4 cards

East ~ Raphael's message of new insight to gain

South ~ Michael's message of where to focus healing

West ~ Gabriel's message of where your emotions may be out of balance

North ~ Uriel's message of what most likely will manifest

I love meditating with the angels. They have a beautiful, light and soft vibration. They are the perfect quick pick me up.

Ascended Masters

Ascended Masters are souls/human beings who have achieved self-mastery while having a physical experience as a human. They lived ordinary lives, yet were able to achieve enlightenment in the physical. Many believe the Ascended Masters are helping humanity to evolve by allowing themselves to be accessible for guidance and assistance.

Some of the well-known Masters are Jesus, Buddha, Kwan Yin, Sanat Kumara, Babaji, and Saint Germain. You may work with one master specifically, or by choice you may work with several. I personally do not work or meditate frequently with the Ascended Masters. I am, however, receptive to whoever chooses to visit with me.

All of these spiritual helpers are part of our consciousness. They always bring through messages of love and inspiration. They are never judgmental or hurtful. If a guide or angel is criticizing you for your actions or making you feel unworthy, chances are you are not connecting to a guide or angel. This can happen if you are not clear and haven't created sacred space.

My last bit of advice regarding working with spiritual helpers is to enjoy connecting, listening, and inviting these beings of light into your life. Do so with an open mind and heart. There is always the danger of becoming co-dependent or possibly losing sight or focus of your physical reality. It is always a good idea to have your own reality checks once in a while, which is why I always suggest working with a soul coach or spiritual mentor

CHAKRAS

The word *Chakra* is a Sanskrit word meaning *spinning wheel*. There are over 100 chakra centers in the body. We are going to focus on the main seven chakras. If even one of your chakras is closed or unbalanced, you may experience fatigue, illness, and mental or an emotional drain. These are just a few possibilities if your chakras are off balance. On the other hand, if your chakras are balanced, open and flowing, you may experience mental clarity, increased stamina, excellent sleep patterns, or even increased intuition.

There are people who are able to see these energy centers and/or feel if a chakra is opened or not. Technology is available to validate or view the chakra system with a camera or computer. I do recommend every once in a while scheduling a chakra balancing session, and even having your aura photographed once a year. Our chakras are energy centers that are constantly moving and changing. Therefore, you may receive a different result in testing your chakras each time they are tested. Regular maintenance and testing are highly desirable.

Chakras 1, 2, and 3 govern the body, desire, will, and emotions. Keep these three balanced, grounded, and clear. They are the foundation as you build energy, much like the foundation of a house. You do want to build energy. The stronger the foundation, the more you can build upon energetically. Self-love is very important to have in place. The 4th chakra connects the lower self with the higher self. This is where psychic energy begins. Love is at the center here. Chakras 5, 6, and 7 concentrate on psychic energy and gifts as well as connection to Source.

Root/*Muladhara* ~ The root chakra is associated with family, love, and social relationships.

- **Location** ~ from the hips down to the feet, the base of the spine. A conelike vortex that starts at the base of the spine and gets wider as it reaches the feet.
- **Color** ~ Red
- **Food** ~ red meat, coffee (caffeine), spinach (iron foods), sugar, and spicy foods like peppers
- **Oil** ~ sandalwood, ginger, cedar, and black pepper
- **Crystals** ~ smoky quartz, red jasper, ruby, tiger's eye, black tourmaline, and hematite
- **Recommended Activities** ~ Meditation, prayers, charity, and selfless sharing.

Sacral/*Swadhisthana* ~ The sacral chakra is connected with creativity, sexuality, and fertility (new beginnings, creative endeavors)

- **Location** ~ a circle in front of the reproductive area as well as behind the body. The spleen area.
- **Color** ~ Orange
- **Food** ~ chocolate, banana, watermelon, milk and other dairy products, and pastas
- **Oil** ~ patchouli, jasmine, damiana and ylang ylang
- **Crystal** ~ carnelian, orange calcite, and sunstone
- **Recommended Activities** ~ creative activities (painting, writing, and/ or working with music), working with your senses, aromatherapy.

Solar Plexus/*Manipura* ~ The solar plexus is the center of our emotions, gut feelings, intuition, and our will center.

- **Location** ~ Located in the stomach area -- in front of the stomach, through the body, as well as behind this region.
- **Color** ~ Yellow
- **Food** ~ carrots, sweet potatoes, fish, chicken, and oranges
- **Oil** ~ rosemary, lemon, ginger, and basil
- **Crystal** ~ citrine, yellow obsidian, apatite, and yellow calcite
- **Recommended Activities** ~ Allowing emotions to flow safely through you. Meditation with deep breathing. Use your willpower to resist a negative pattern or activity.

Heart/*Anahata* ~ The heart chakra is the center or our physical, emotional, mental, and spiritual bodies. This is our center to connect to Divine, to self, and to relationship love.

- **Location** ~ In front of, through, and behind the physical heart.
- **Color** ~ Green or Pink
- **Food** ~ cherries, strawberries, greens, and grains.
- **Oil** ~ rose, lavender, and hibiscus
- **Crystal** ~ rose quartz, jade, garnet, and emerald
- **Recommended Activities** ~ Write a love letter to yourself, list 100 good qualities you have, and work on forgiveness of self and others.

Throat/*Vissudha* ~ The communication center and/or creative expression.

- **Location** ~ In front of and behind the throat, neck, mouth, and ears.
- **Color** ~ Light Blue
- **Food** ~ wheat grass, blueberries, kelp, and Echinacea
- **Oil** ~ chamomile, bayberry, benzoin, and wisteria
- **Crystal** ~ turquoise, blue lace agate, and lapis lazuli
- **Recommended Activities** ~ Learning to speak your truth either through journaling or automatic writing and singing.

Third Eye/*Ajna* ~ The third eye chakra is the center for clairvoyance, the ability to clearly see the future.

- **Location** ~ In front of as well as through and behind the forehead, the pineal gland, the eyes, and nose.
- **Color** ~ Purple
- **Food** ~ water, lecithin, dandelion, and alfalfa
- **Oil** ~ clary sage, blue yarrow, mugwort, and frankincense
- **Crystal** ~ fluorite, amethyst, lapis lazuli, and pietersite
- **Recommended Activities** ~ Meditation, psychic development activities, and chanting mantras such as *ohm*.

Crown/*Sahasnrana*** ~** The crown chakra connects you with your higher source, higher realms, and divinity.

- **Location** ~ a conelike vortex spinning from the top of the head upward.
- **Color** ~ White/Indigo
- **Food** ~ water, green tea
- **Oil** ~ myrrh, sandalwood, and frankincense
- **Crystal** ~ sugilite, elestial, diamond, and lemurian seed crystal
- **Recommended Activities** ~ Meditation, prayer, and spiritual studies.

Simple and Easy Chakra Activities

Pendulum ~ There are two exercises I use with my chakra work. Any pendulum will work.

Chakra Test

Begin by holding your pendulum about 3 inches from the root chakra in front of the body. Allow the pendulum to move naturally. Ideally the pendulum would swing in a clockwise manner. If this does occur, then the chakra is open and flowing in a healthy way. If the chakra is not moving or has a wobbly motion, it is out of balance. It may be over stimulated or under stimulated. Yes, overstimulation means too much energy is moving in that center. If this is the case, it can energetically throw us out of balance. You would continue moving the pendulum up the body and finishing with the crown over the head. This is a great way to test to see if your chakras are balanced and open. If they are not, you would begin the next exercise.

Chakras are energy centers; they are always changing. You may be open and balanced one day and then the next be out of balance in different areas.

Chakra Balancing With The Pendulum

You may balance the chakras by simply holding a pendulum over the chakra. I am always careful to move into the energy center in a careful way. Sudden, quick movements into anyone's auric field can be disturbing. We all know how it feels when someone gets in our personal space with jerky movements. It can be uncomfortable. As you hold the pendulum about three inches from the chakra, you may bring in the visualization of the corresponding color as well as holding the pendulum in the same chakra until it moves clockwise in a smooth and flowing circle. You will intuitively know when it is time to move to the next chakra. After you have finished with the crown chakra (over your head or over the receiver's head), you have completed the balancing.

Toning ~ Aligning and clearing the chakras may be achieved simply by toning the Sanskrit name for each chakra while placing your hands on the corresponding chakra.

- Root ~ *Muladhara*
- Sacral ~ *Swadhisthana*
- Solar Plexus ~ *Manipura*
- Heart ~ *Anahata*
- Throat ~ *Visshudha*
- Third Eye ~ *Ajna*
- Crown ~ *Sahasrana*

Color Therapy ~ Each of the chakras has, as mentioned above, a corresponding color. By integrating color correspondence, you can align, balance, and strengthen the chakra. You do this by placing the appropriate colored stone on the area of the body for the chakra with which you are working. You could wear the color of the chakra you are choosing to work with that day. For example, if I would like to strengthen my throat chakra and work on my communication skills, then I might wear the color blue, wear a blue necklace, maybe wear one with turquoise, place a blue crystal in my pocket, or for the ladies in my bra (yes, bra!).

- I have also burned specific colored candles to help remind me I am balancing and strengthening that chakra.
- You might create an altar dedicated to a certain chakra. For the solar plexus you might use yellow candles, yellow crystals, lemons, etc. to create an altar dedicated to the solar plexus.

Tuning Forks ~ Using a tuning fork through sound vibrational therapy can help align the chakras. After using the striker to start the vibration of your tuning fork, place the end of the fork on each chakra.

Reiki/Energy Work/Healing ~ Receiving any type of energy healing will help get those chakras in shape, leaving you feeling energized, more optimistic, and balanced. There are many modalities out there.

Please use your intuition and the referral system when seeking energetic healing. There are a lot of energy practitioners. I am always selective about whom I allow to work on me.

Hands Clockwise and Counterclockwise ~ You may perform this modality on others as well as yourself.

- Begin by warming up your hands to turn them on by rubbing them together.
- Take your opened left hand with the palm facing the body, hold it over the root chakra, move the hand counterclockwise several rotations. While circling the

- body counterclockwise, envision the palm as a magnet picking up particles of stuck energy like metal filings.
- When you feel as if you have pulled the energy completely, brush the hands together, blow the energy off your cupped hands with a cleansing deep breath, and release the energy.
- Move your right hand over the root clockwise until you feel the chakra is full, balanced, and complete.
- Brush/rub both hands together, blow on your cupped hands, and release the energy.
- Now move to the next chakra, in this case the sacral chakra. Begin the process again with the left hand as a magnet.
- The final chakra, the crown, is above the head. Work in the area above the head following the same protocol, left hand first.
- When finished, draw a figure 8 across and along the body to balance the energetic meridians of the body, to form a reconnection of left and right, male and female energy.

Sound Crystal Bowls Or Ringing A Bell ~ Sound vibrational therapy is a wonderful way to balance your chakras. The vibration moves through the body, aligning the entire auric field, not just the chakras. You may achieve this effect with not only with the crystal bowls, but also with a drum, a bell, a rattle or a flute - all will work just as well.

Meditation

- *Breathe, relax, and close your eyes. Bring your awareness to the base of your spine. Your attention is now on the root chakra. See this spinning cone of energy at the base of your spine spinning slowly and evenly clockwise. The cone touches the earth and is emitting a clear red color into your aura with the sense of a solid foundation, great healthy relationships, and groundedness.*

- *Next, move on up to your sacral chakra. This center is located in the* hip area. See the color orange. See a wheel of orange spinning clockwise from the front of your body through to the back, slowly and evenly bringing in feelings of passion and fertility.

- We now move up to the solar plexus with a wheel of yellow spinning in front of your stomach area through to the back of the body with a feeling of self-respect and strong willpower to follow through with your intentions.

- Next, move up a little further to the heart center with the color green spinning in front of your chest through to the back of the chest with love vibration in and from your heart.

- We now move on to the throat area, the color of sky blue in our wheel of energy, flowing in front of your throat center all the way through and behind the neck, and envisioning healthy communication and creativity.

- After the throat chakra, we move up to the third eye center, which is located in the middle of your forehead. The color of purple is sent out from this intuitive center with clear psychic vision, seeing clearly beyond the veil of illusion. This wheel spins in front of the body as well as behind to the back of the head.

- Finally, we move to the top of the head, the crown chakra. Iridescent white light spins through this center above the head like a cone, bringing in clear connection with our higher mind, our higher guidance.

- As these wheels all spin, they are clearing energy and sending this energy down through the body, out through the bottoms of your feet, into the *earth to be recycled for new growth, new beginning. Enjoy the visual of all your wheels turning and spinning in a healthy manner for a few moments.*

- *When you are ready, open your eyes.*

I encourage everyone to make the time to balance your chakras on a daily basis. It only takes a few moments, yet the long-term results of healthier and happier lives are worth the time and energy invested.

Seeing Auras

A simple way of seeing the auric field around a person is really quite simple.

Tools ~ An open mind, a light, solid-colored background (such as white, tan, or beige) that is neutral colored, medium lighting

- Have someone stand in front of the wall. I would also encourage them to wear neutral, solid colored clothing.
- Stand or sit six feet away from them and look at them with your eyes in a relaxed gaze. Focus on the center or their body, slowly work your way to the outline of their body. Stay in a relaxed gaze, and then move your gaze to the outline of their body, maybe 2 inches from the body. You should start to see colors coming off of the body. This does take practice, trust the colors you see. You might even feel the colors (for example warmth or a tingly feeling).

Document your experience.

Laurie Barraco

CHANNELING

Channeling is allowing guidance, energy, and wisdom from another entity which can be higher self, guides, the God consciousness, angels etc. to flow to you or through you.

We all channel, it is the stream of consciousness which flows through us. We have all randomly said things without knowing where it comes from. We often channel or receive information either for ourselves or others through spiritual collectives. A spiritual collective is what I see as your non-physical help. This includes higher self, guides, angels, deceased loved ones, as well as the other non-physical entities that work with you personally (ex. Masters of Light, etc.)

What is channeling? The common idea of channeling is an experience in which one completely loses oneself to a separate entity being channeled (a.k.a "trance channeling"), it is not the only, nor even the ideal, form of channeling. Trance channeling bypasses the individual, thus limiting the individual's opportunity to learn and grow through the experience.

- **Trance Channeling:** A form of mediumship where an individual will relinquish conscious control of his body and give it over to an "outside entity" for use as an instrument of communication. During these sessions, the channel has no knowledge or recollection of what is happening. He or she simply "goes away"

and then becomes awakened when his body is fatigued or when the session is over.
- **Conscious Channeling:** A form of mediumship where the channel maintains conscious presence but agrees to allow expression of truths or images originating from another entity to come through his physical body. At any time the channel is free to edit the material being presented, or to refuse expression when he or she is not comfortable with the information that is being offered.
- **Automatic Writing, Painting, Or Musicianship:** A form of mediumship where the channel (either in trance or consciously) allows his body to use any one of a number of artistic venues to express the ideas or emotions of an entity that exists outside of his or her immediate life context.

Edgar Cayce often emphasized the importance of attuning to the Higher Self, while remaining conscious.

In this way, any person can channel the higher self, while at the same time access his or her own individual creativity and heightened experience of connection with the universe while remaining an individual. In its broadest sense, channeling includes any act of transmission, whether of love (as in giving someone a hug); an idea (as in sharing it with someone); creative effort; and many other forms.

When we have an intuitive hunch regarding something we should or shouldn't do, this is a form of channeled guidance. There are countless anecdotes concerning intuitive guidance, as well as scientific evidence for the efficacy of following such guidance.

Here are some basic principles to remember in developing intuition:

Why Channel?

1. To receive information and wisdom to learn
2. To bring through messages of validation and comfort

To prove that you are super-psychic, gifted, or a "chosen one" are not valid reasons. I know I repeat myself but humility, integrity, and with the intention of what is for the highest and best good for all are so important!

Well Known Channels ~ Jane Roberts, Esther Hicks, Edgar Cayce, Elizabeth Claire Prophet, Jacqueline T. Snyder, Lorraine Smith and Candyce Strafford. I also channel, but it is not a trance channel.

Guidelines

- Creating the space, sage, incense, crystals
- Being in a sacred space within, absolutely no substances, yes some use psychedelics, but I do not suggest these
- Prayers ~ hand motions, mudras etc. also help one open up to guidance
- Protection
- Motives
- Not to be played with, not to experiment, serious business
- Does take discipline.
- By using the conditioning, it can help you get into the state of mind
- Warning - just because someone channels, it does not mean they are more highly evolved. There have been people whom I question from where the information is coming. It may be valid at first, but then the trickster aspect comes through.
- An entity is not necessarily more evolved if it is in spirit form. Proof and trust need to be built.

Some people experience more than one voice or presence trying to communicate with them. I would suggest you work with your filter (higher self) to help with a more orderly process. You can also ask the group to communicate as a collective, or ask if there is a spokesperson.

Suggested Questions To Ask While Channeling

Here are a few sample questions to ask whether communicating with an angel, your higher self, guides, crossed over loved ones, masters of light, a spiritual collective:

- Who are you?
- Is there a name I can call you?
- What are you here to teach me?
- What obstacles am I overlooking?

If channeling interests you, I highly, highly recommend that you do not rush into it. Take your time, find a reputable mentor and make sure you are taking the proper precautions (mentioned in the guidelines). Carelessly opening yourself to etheric energies can be detrimental to your soul.

If you take your time and allow the process to unfold slowly with caution, you will have profound soul growth and clarity. Don't forget to journal all of your experiences ~ you'll be glad you did!

REINCARNATION

The area of reincarnation/past lives is fascinating to many people, and I would like to share what I have learned about the topic. How many lives have I had? What was I in my past life? I am asked these questions on a daily basis, and I am more than happy to assist people with their answers. I do prefer to help them to discover who they were and how having a little bit of information can help them in this lifetime.

Why do we come back and back and back again? Simply put, we gain knowledge, wisdom, and experience for the soul. The choices and actions we make and take in our lives accept our consciousness. This is how the soul grows through trials and tribulations as well as how we treat others and how we overcome adversity. There is no better way to transform the soul to a higher consciousness/vibration.

By living in different cultures and experiencing difficulties and extremes, we become well-seasoned souls. We have all been male and female over and over again. Each soul takes time to select the best environments for its growth in each given lifetime. Parents, geographical locations, birth order, sex, culture, and time are all are taken carefully into consideration. Often we disregard patterns and overlook tendencies and challenging relationships as merely coincidences or annoyances. We hurry to move through these events and relationships. The stimuli have all been carefully selected for growth. The conditions are perfect for all of us. This is why I encourage people to pay attention to everything in their lives. Try not to overanalyze, but pay attention. Everything and everyone is significant, even if it is a brief relationship or what may seem to be an insignificant interaction. All is perfect and purposeful.

Reincarnation

My belief is we are energy, souls of light, and we carefully choose or select when, how, why, and where to take physical bodies for learning for the soul's growth. Everything in your life is purposeful. Your parents, gifts, interests, etc. are carefully planned before you come into each lifetime. We can be spirit guides to help people and learn through secondhand guiding or receive firsthand life experience by living here on Earth.

How Many Different Lives Do People Have?

I have experienced in sessions that most people have lived thousands of lives and have had experiences in almost every imaginable circumstance. They have been a part of various cultures, lived as male and female, mother and son, Asian, Russian, Indian - you name it.

Do We Ever Stop Incarnating?

Sure, we do stop incarnating at some point, and we do rest in between existences. Also, I encourage people not to feel bad for his or her past life experiences. Some people say they must have been a terrible person in another lifetime. This may be the case, but you are here now to correct undesirable behavior, to do it all over in a different more conscious way of living. Simply put, you are here for a do-over.

How Can I Find Out About My Past Lives?

There are many ways to uncover and learn about your past lives.

You can try the following:

- Consult with a trusted psychic/intuitive.
- Go within with meditation.
- Try automatic writing/journaling by asking questions and allowing the answers to flow through your pen or pencil. I would encourage you to have questions prepared ahead of time to help you.
- Schedule a Past Life Regression with a trained professional.
- Listen to a guided meditation. Brian Weiss' work is wonderful as well as Dick Sutphen's.
- Pay attention to dreams. Sometimes we have glimpses in our dream state of people, scenery, and eras. These can be sneak peaks into the past.

Suggestions

I feel that I need to put a few pointers here regarding Reincarnation and Past Lives.

- The most important lifetime is the one you are living now. You have blinders on because the veil of forgetfulness has been created so that we can focus on one lifetime at a time. You are here to grow as the personality reading these words. I will say it again in a different way. Who you were before is not nearly as important as whom you are now. You are here to experience. The past life existences do affect you in this lifetime, and at the same time, this lifetime affects those lifetimes.
- With past life recall, you can heal unfounded phobias, negative traits, and negative karmic contracts simply by correcting your behavior now. Hypnosis and counseling are only a few remedies for past life overflow.
- Make sure the information and story "feels" right to you. A past life reader may say they see a certain lifetime and you aren't sure it resonates. Then don't make it part of your story. Just because someone sees it does not mean that what they say is accurate. It could even be that specific lifetime recall isn't significant in this lifetime. Trust yourself.
- An accurate reader/recaller would be able to give you specifics. For example, they might say your mother was a sister in a past lifetime and that the two of you competed over men in Italy. If

this information makes sense as to why there were some odd competitive behaviors between your Mother and yourself and you love all things Italian, this might be an accurate recall.
- A shamanic journey with a trained shaman can help you journey with the elements into the earth to help you recall and heal fragmented lifetimes. This is often referred to as Soul Retrieval. I do encourage you to do your research and to find someone who is highly recommended to assist with this area. It can be a very profound experience. Some even believe people with schizophrenia have very thin veils and are experiencing different personalities filtering into this lifetime.

In cases of mental illness, it is best to work with trained professionals

Have We Been With The People In Previous Lives Who Are Now In Our Lives?

Yes, most everyone in your life has agreed to play certain parts or help you learn certain key points about yourself. This also includes the challenging people. We are part of soul groups. You have selected them from a past life to help you grow here on Earth in this particular existence.

What About Animals?

Animals do reincarnate. I have had the same dog soul come back to me. You can recognize the soul through the eyes. This is also true with animals.

Can People Come Back As Animals Or Plants?

If we have been extremely selfish in a lifetime, we may spend some time as a rock or tree. They have the least amount of desire for the self. After we are complete with that understanding, the soul energy moves up the consciousness ladder so to speak.

Meditation To Past Life As An American Indian

Through thousands of readings over the years, I have noticed one common past lifetime experience. Everyone has experience with at least one lifetime as a Native American Indian. With this meditation you may read ahead, follow the meditation through memory, ask someone else to guide you through the meditation, or record it beforehand.

Tools

Drumming or Native American music playing in the background, a woodsy oil blend such as the Young Living Blend Sacred Mountain, sage, candle, 4 stones (one to place in each of the four directions east, south, west and north), a crystal to connect with past lives, a journal, and a pen or pencil. You will journal your experience when the meditation is finished.

Meditation

- *Close your eyes and relax. Let's take some cleansing breaths in and out through the nose and mouth. As you breathe, you become more and more relaxed. As you continue to breathe, focus your attention on your breathing and go to your heart center. Within your heart center you are able to journey and travel to other lifetimes and wisdom. As you look more deeply into your heart, you are suddenly surrounded by trees and are in the middle of an open field.*

- *You look around; everything you see, hear, feel, or smell is valid and you will remember.*

- *In this open field you notice a circle of stones. Step inside; again*

- *you will remember everything about this experience. You sit down in the center of this circle. You cross your legs, and you close your eyes. Breathe in your surroundings.*

- *As you sit here quietly inside this medicine wheel, you review one of your lifetimes as a Native American Indian. Allow yourself to experience this life now.*

- *It is now time for you to rise and step out of the wheel. Your focus goes again to your heart center. You slowly become more aware of your body. When you are ready, open your eyes.*

How Do I Choose To Use The Information From My Past Lives?

In my own personal self-discovery of past lives, I have found I have had many lives here on Earth. I have been a little of everything and have been everywhere.

When I keep seeing signs which have a certain theme, such as all things Native American which might include feathers, drums, or the buffalo, I know it is time to get out my drumming music or to do my own drumming. I might even grab my Medicine Cards by Jamie Samms for a reading. To me, this may mean it is time to tap into that lifetime and bring through some wisdom my soul has gained from that lifetime experience.

These days I have a lot of influence from an Egyptian lifetime. I was decorating the new store in all things Egyptian, from a 6+ foot sarcophagus to the red and gold accents. Where do I go from there? Well, I might work with the Egyptian deities. For example, I might call in Thoth to assist with this book. He was the scribe who helped people write their ideas down on papyrus. You need to pay attention in your own life to signs that may show a connection to a past life.

Please do not use this information I have shared for your healing and growth as a distraction from healing during this lifetime. Remember that the lifetime you are presently experiencing is the one which is of the utmost importance.

Laurie Barraco

MEDIUMSHIP

Mediumship is the ability to communicate with souls, entities, and personalities which no longer have a physical body. We all have the capacity to communicate with the deceased. The key to receiving and connecting depends upon your own frequency/vibration. Mediumship is a wonderful gift that can bring healing and reconnection. Meditation is the best way to calm the mind and fine tune the intuition. By developing your intuition, bringing in discipline, and taking your time with your process, you will be able to trust the messages from those who have crossed over with ease and comfort.

I know and have heard many stories, myths, and fears people have shared with me regarding the subject of mediumship. I have heard it all!

Spirits communicate in many different ways. No two are alike. I have seen lights flicker, specific songs played at strategic times, and coins show up in the most interesting places. By the way, always check the year of the coin. It usually is a marker for a specific birth, anniversary, etc. I have also seen feathers show up unexpectedly. I could go on and on with examples. Spirits all have different calling cards. Just be sure you are not discrediting the message and signs. It is not easy to transcend dimensions! They are working hard to help validate for us. They do not need to reveal themselves for the spirit world. The light shows and performances are all for us in the physical world who need validation and reassurance.

Myth ~ It is taboo to communicate with the dead, or my faith/religion says it is bad to go to people who do this for a living.

Facts ~ There are many misconceptions in the area of what is right and wrong spiritually. If you are working with your heart for the good of all without consciously trying to manipulate or control anyone, it is not wrong to communicate with the other side. I will not preach in this area. I do believe we all have the right to practice spiritually where we feel our most comfortable. I do think religion may be limited to certain teachings, methods, and beliefs. I also know what works for some may not work for others.

There are rituals and prayers that I use from my Catholic background, but do I follow these by the book? No. I use what resonates and leave behind what does not. This is a personal preference, and I encourage all people to work with and use what feels right to them as individuals.

Almost all of the messages are of validation that spirits made it to the Light and are not suffering anymore. They also love to validate the signs they give to the living to prove they are still with them (for example - certain songs being played on the radio, finding tokens or feathers in unique places). Often they show me flashes of events that have just occurred to show they witness your celebrations and your sorrows.

I only can share from my experience, and not once through thousands of sessions have I witnessed a spirit being upset with someone for communicating with them. I encourage you to weigh the pros and cons and to request to be healed of any and all negative beliefs regarding the other side.

Myth ~ All mediums are psychic, but not all psychics are mediums.

Fact ~ True, not all psychics are able to make the connection with the other side. In fact, there are some psychics who prefer not to communicate with the deceased for their own personal reasons. They may not feel comfortable with the process because of their own personal beliefs, or some may not have strong mediumship abilities. If psychics are unable to connect with the other side, it does not mean they are not gifted. Each person's psychic abilities are individually unique.

Myth ~ If you try to communicate with the deceased, you are holding them back and pulling them out of the Light.

Fact ~ We are multidimensional beings. We are already communicating with them whether we are conscious of the communication or not. Our soul is much more than this physical body. For example when we sleep, we leave our bodies. A small part of our soul essence stays with the physical body to keep it going, but our soul travels for learning and visiting other souls alive and deceased. We go on a spiritual walkabout when we sleep and meditate.

When we communicate with the deceased, we are communicating with a fraction of their soul entity; therefore, we are not holding them back. We are actually helping them evolve as they assist us in evolving our souls.

Myth ~ Do the spirits hold grudges?

Fact ~ It is my experience that the deceased do not usually hold grudges. They are more focused on healing and repairing the harm that has been created by their doing. Grudges are human/egotistical traits, which are not usually held by evolved soul entities.

Myth ~ He/She wasn't a nice person to me. I do not want to hear from that person.

Fact ~ Most, I won't say all, but most souls are counseled and go through a process of understanding where they could have made different choices. They are also shown how they made others feel. For example they experience the pain they have caused others by experiencing it themselves. As they go through this review, their soul entities are elevated to higher spiritual planes of existence. As their frequency is raised, the negative personality traits start to morph or shift to a more loving perspective or understanding.

Myth ~ He/She was such a bad person. I am sure they are not in a "good" place.

Fact ~ It is of the utmost importance when souls cross over for them to be counseled and shown how they could have lived differently. There are different choices they could have made. There are also different entry levels of consciousness when we cross over. Where we are consciously before we pass is where we enter in as we cross over. For example, some leave the earth plane at middle school level spiritually/consciously; therefore, they enter into middle school in the etheric realms. If you evolve your soul to, say a college level, then when you cross over, you enter at a more blissful state of existence. Get the idea? Even as we leave our bodies behind, we still grow and evolve in the afterlife.

I don't know about you, but I am going to keep working at being the most loving, caring, sharing, authentic, inspiring being I can be here on Earth!

Myth ~ We do not have the right to contact them.

Fact ~ Anyone and everyone has the ability to connect with souls who have crossed over. When we aspire to connect with them, we are connecting with the personality we knew. Their soul is multi-dimensional.

We are only contacting and communicating with a small fraction of their being. It does concern me when people aren't able to make decisions and are distracted or obsessed with what the deceased would have said or done. They have moved on and are for the most part in a different "mode" of consciousness. They are not worried or bothered by our human trivial concerns (for example: I was not able to sing at her funeral, or I was not able to bear a son to carry on the family name).

They see the bigger picture. Their message is always, "Appreciate the beauty and joys of the physical world. Say I am sorry when necessary, and forgive and forget often." They also say quite frequently, "It really doesn't matter does it?"

What Can Developing My Mediumship Abilities Do For Me?

- You will learn about life after death. This can help those who fear the other side and lessen the anxiety about the afterlife.
- To help yourself as well as others move through grief and pain. By communicating with the crossed over loved ones, we see they are not suffering anymore and that they are in a better place.
- To bring in closure, if closure wasn't an option. Often in readings there is closure and understanding of why and how these people reacted or behaved while they were alive. This helps the deceased, as well as, those who are still alive move on without guilt. Mostly, this is for those living. We do not have the overall perspective as those in spirit, so they are not hanging on to guilt as much as we do here on Earth. Guilt is a physical and egotistical human emotion.
- To open up communication with the Spirit world. There is much to learn and comprehend. We can receive knowledge that we don't have access to while here on Earth.

Creating The Space For Medium Communication

- The room is private, quiet, softly lit, and clutter-free.
- Sit in a comfortable chair.
- Relax the body with deep breathing exercises.
- Clear the mind.
- Take time to reach a comfort level.

- Connect with your higher self/spirit guide.
- Let the higher self know what you are respectfully requesting - the questions.
- See and feel the vision.
- Use your common sense and reason about what you are feeling, seeing, and in some cases what you are hearing. Often you will smell some different aromas in the room.
- Don't force the answers, let the information flow, flow, flow.
- Verbalize to the client or yourself the stream or flow of what is transpiring. Never break up the continuity of information by asking if you are on the mark.
- Try not to control the session with ultimatums, demands, or with expecting miraculous signs from them.
- Do not try to interpret the information. Often the clarity comes in at a later time and date. The psychic opening of energy is present; you don't want to waste time with trivial details.
- When you are complete with the session, be sure to thank the spirits!

A New Prayer ~

I ask for strength and to be guided by the White Light. Please protect me with this White Light as I open myself to contact with non-physical entities. You may like to repeat this prayer three times.

Questions To Ask

- Who are you?
- What is your name?
- Are you related?
- What is your message?
- What caused your passing?
- What are your signs/signals?
- Are you helping with anything specifically?

Suggested Techniques To Communicate

I have listed a few techniques to help you become more comfortable with your intuition, as well as, bringing in the other side. Before using any technique, please take the time to create your sacred space. I am sure you are familiar with this protocol by now. I suggest extreme caution. Make sure your higher self-filter is in place to help screen the energies coming through.

- Visualize a large imaginary room in your house, a very private room that is also a movie screening room. Arrange the theater seats, a stage, curtain, sound system, decorate and paint this room. You sit down in your private theater, raise the curtain, dim the lights, and bring your focus to the screen on the wall. Remember to take your time creating this private screening room. With this method, you should be able to see and hear activities on this screen. You might need to adjust the focus or volume. Let the scene unfold and listen to the messages.
    When the transmission of energy and information is complete, be sure to thank the visitor(s) and open the space. Be sure to journal your answers, if at all possible.

- Another technique is using automatic writing as a way for the energy to work through you.
- I would suggest creating the space and being as centered and open as possible.
- Have the questions prepared ahead of time.
- Use your relaxation technique of breathing and expansion.
- When you are relaxed, start writing a correspondence to the spirit entity with whom you wish to communicate. If you do not have anyone in mind, simply allow the pen to flow on the paper.
- I read the questions out loud, and then answer without thinking or censoring the information. This works for some, but not everyone.
- Of course there is always the plain, old, regular meditation route. You allow thoughts and the energy to flow naturally. Sometimes spirits come to visit in my daily meditation. You never know who is going to show up.

Mediumship is one of the most popular subjects about which I am asked. When people inquire about mediumship, I always encourage them to take their time, practice, do spiritual work, and allow the process to flow naturally. Try not to force the process. By forcing it you may be missing a few necessary steps in the evolution of your psychic development (for example: learning how to protect yourself from unwanted psychic energy).

Honestly, it is not necessary to work very hard at mediumship. Loved ones are revealing themselves to us constantly. As with all areas of psychic development, I encourage you to know your limits, protect yourself energetically, and enjoy the natural process. Don't forget to journal your experiences.

PSYCHOMETRY

What Is Psychometry?

Psychometry is using your sense of touch to feel the impressions, imprints, or vibrations of a physical object. We are able to pick up impressions, messages, feelings, and more. All physical matter has energy imprinted on it.

Most of us have had the experience of shopping at yard sales and consignment stores. There may be a certain good that was appealing to sight, yet when you picked it up, you instinctively put it back. You used your sense of psychometry to feel the vibration of the object and sensed it did not match your frequency.

Receptive Hand ~ Use your receptive hand when using psychometry.

Which is the receptive hand? That is the less dominant hand. I am left-handed; therefore, I would use my right hand.

How About A Little Test?

1. Hold both hands at chest level with fingertips pointing up and palms facing each other.

2. Rub hands together very lightly to stimulate the energy flow.

3. Move your hands apart, closer together, then apart, feeling the flow of energy.

4. Whichever hand feels stronger or is emitting stronger energy is your dominant hand. The other is your non-dominant or receptive hand. Always use your receptive hand in psychometry.

When you are beginning your work in psychometry, always pick up or touch an object with your receptive hand. If you pick up the object with your dominant hand, you may inadvertently transmit an impression as you do.

Form a habit of using your receptive hand to take things from others and to pick up something you may intend to use. This will be a challenge in psychometry because you are probably used to picking things up and holding them with your dominant hand, but this practice will help you to remember to use your receptive hand for psychometric work.

Turn On Those Hands

A quick and easy way of warming up is to rub the hands together. It does awaken the hand chakras. (Yes, there are chakras in your hands.)

After a while you will condition your hands to turn on in this way. Is it necessary to rub them together? No, but it works for many people.

Aside From Readings, When Can I Use Psychometry?

- Use it to see which foods feel right for you.
- When out shopping for furniture, clothes, cars, etc.

- When selecting a pet - don't laugh. Don't we usually pet or hold the animal?
- For healing, has anyone ever said, "feel this (ex. A bump)". What do you do? You feel it to see what comes to you.
- When purchasing crystals, I hand select them to energetically "see" how they feel whenever possible.

I could go on and on, but you get the idea of where I am going with the usage of psychometry.

Exercises ~ most of these exercises are more effective with a partner or in a group setting.

What Is In The Envelope?

Supplies ~ a security envelope (or one you cannot see through) a pen, and an object only you have owned, touched, or had in your possession.

- Privately place an object in the envelope, seal it, and give it to your partner. If you are in a group setting, make a little marking in one of the corners so you know it is yours.
- Pass around the envelopes. Each person receives one. If only two people are present, switch envelopes.
- Write down your impressions of what the object is on one side of the envelope. Write it all down - names, colors, feelings, possibly fragrances, messages, etc. Do not worry about being right or wrong.
- If you are in a group setting, see if you can guess the owner of the envelope.
- Share your experience by reading out loud your written information.

This is a fun exercise you can do over and over again. It will most certainly help build your psychometry skills.

Creating Crystal Links With Psychometry

Supplies - pairs of the same crystals (ex. rose quartz, hematite). If you are in a group setting, you will need several different types of pairs of crystals.

If you are working in a pair with someone, only one set of crystals is needed. Rose quartz or two of any crystal will do because all of them are energy transmitters.

If working in a group setting, I encourage you to use a bowl to hold all the crystals in one place. Pass around the bowl. Everyone will select a crystal with eyes closed. That way you won't know what color you have or who has the match.

Meditation To Connect With The Crystal and The Energetic Link To The Other Person.

- *Hold the crystal in your receptive hand, then switch. Get comfortable, relax, and breathe...the crystal becomes warmer in your hand and comes alive.*

- *Allow your hand to feel the pulsing energy from the crystal. As the pulsating energy builds, allow it to connect with its twin in the room. You can feel the flow to and from the person in the room. As you create an infinity flow, you send and receive information, impressions, visions, and feelings. Allow the crystal to form a bond between you and the person holding the twin. Allow time to create this bond to do a reading.*

Write all of your impressions down. If you are working in a group setting, guess who has the twin. This exercise is a favorite and a lot of fun. Share the messages you received.

Last Tip To Open Up Your Senses

By now, you are becoming more and more aware of abilities you never knew you had. We have strong energy centers in our hands, fingertips, and palms. Why not, with intention, awaken the energy centers in your fingers and palms to become more sensitive to the vibrations all around you with your sense of touch?

The next time you go into a meditation, place your hands on your thighs, palms up, and request to have your energy centers open at the appropriate time and place and to be more sensitive only if it is in your best interest. This only needs to be done once. You may notice an increase of the tingly feeling. Remember, everyone feels energy differently. It will help your success rate if you do not compare with others.

Laurie Barraco

ANIMAL COMMUNICATION AND ANIMAL TOTEMS

In this next chapter, I will discuss the subject of animals. Animals have been sharing this Earth journey with us since the beginning of time. They bring us comfort, companionship, love, protection, service, messages, and healing. We often receive confirmations of ideas, thoughts, and affirmations of which direction to go next.

I have been known to look up the meaning of a particular animal after it shows up for me. I will research the meaning online as well as refer to my *Animal Speak* book by Ted Andrews. The message can bring us clarity, validation, as well as a teaching. The Native Americans used the animals as signs from the Creator bringing in messages.

Animal Totems and Power Animals

There are different schools of thought regarding animal totems and power animals. After many personal sessions with clients, my own time spent in meditation, and observation of the animals that have crossed my path, I have gained quite a bit of respect for the creatures that swim, fly, and crawl on this beautiful earth.

Power Animals

A power animal is the animal your soul has chosen to be a guiding and teaching influence for the duration of your physical life here on earth. The power animal does not change, and most people have one special animal messenger which has shown itself repeatedly in their lives during crisis, at a crossroads, or as simply a validation of a decision needing to be made.

Is it possible to have more than one power animal? Yes, it is possible, but usually people have one main teaching and protecting animal influence in their lives.

How do you know what your power animal is? This animal usually makes frequent appearances in your life in dreams, out in the physical world, in meditations, or you may have a strong affection or pull towards one type of animal. Usually people already know which power animal is working with them.

Later in this chapter I will guide you through a meditation to help you recognize and bond with your power animal.

Animal Totems

Animal totems are the messengers that come and go in our lives bringing in messages, protection, and inspiration during the different stages of our lives. A simple example is this - you do not need the same teachers throughout your life. We go through stages of evolvement. You would not stay with the same kindergarten teacher throughout your life just as you would not consult a midwife to help build a house.

As we encounter different challenges, opportunities, and growth spurts, we draw to us the help that is needed for our growth. These animals may come several different times in your life as support. A vulture may show up when you are releasing what no longer serves. We do this many times in our lives. Therefore, when the vulture appears, you know you are in a cleansing phase. Makes sense doesn't it? By getting better acquainted with the animals, you will be able to navigate through life with a little more confidence, clarity, and support.

Ways The Animals Reveal Themselves To You

- Dreams
- Meditation
- Journaling, automatic writing
- Oracle, tarot cards
- Out in the world
- Television
- Psychic premonitions
- Gifts
- In books
- Stories

Meditation To Meet Your Power Animal

- *Find a quiet, private place and create sacred space with sage, a candle, soft music if desired, a journal, pen, and/or a recording device. By the way, a leopard jasper stone is wonderful to help you retrieve your power animal.*

- *Begin by slowing down your breathing, slowly inhaling and exhaling. As you continue to become more aware of your breath, breathe in light, then exhale stress and negativity. Your breath is now becoming more rhythmic, relaxing, and your body begins to feel weightless. See yourself expanding and becoming lighter and lighter.*

- *I would like you to bring your focus now to your third eye, the area between the eyes just above your eyebrows. Envision a bubble of light with iridescent colors inside this bubble as well as outside the bubble. Look a little closer at this bubble. As you do, you see another world inside the bubble. This bubble in a way looks like the globes you shake to make snow appear.*

- *This bubble is going to be your transportation which takes you to meet your power animal. See yourself traveling through the air, out of the room, and out of the town. You are arriving at the destination of your power animal's natural environment.*

- *Step out of your bubble. What do you see? Do you see trees, a beach, or the forest? Take a deep breath. What do you smell? Is it warm or cold? Is there water? Are you in the water?*

- *Off to the left you see an obstruction, a wall. Coming out from behind the wall is your power animal. Is it what you thought it would be? Have you seen this animal before? What is its name? What is its purpose, and why is this animal with you? Take time to really get acquainted with your guide.*

- *Pause*

- *It is now time to come back to awareness. You can visit your power animal in this space whenever you so choose. Get back in your bubble to slowly travel back to this room. Step out of the bubble. Come back to this room. Journal your experience.*

Animal Divination Signs

- **Hawk** ~ pay attention to all which is going on in this moment, a teacher, can be a warning, need for quick reassessment
- **Eagle** ~ strong messenger of Great Spirit, you are blessed, protected, and higher consciousness is available to you in this moment
- **Cardinal** ~ father/grandfather figure in spirit revealing himself, strong, confidence, you are in mastery
- **Bluejay** ~ mother/grandmother figure in spirit coming through, soft feminine guidance, family oriented time
- **Dog** ~ loyalty, protection
- **Cat** ~ mystical, astral travel, time for play, independence
- **Spider** ~ weaving the web, all things connected and linking up, storyteller
- **Ladybug** ~ lucky time ahead, the Midas touch
- **Vulture** ~ a time of cleansing and releasing. Releasing is necessary for new to come in
- **Owl** ~ wisdom, nighttime activities, time for education
- **Dragonfly** ~ spirit is all around you, a time of validation of being on the right path for your evolution
- **Wolf** ~ teacher, family support, they live in packs, surround yourself with like-minded people
- **Bear** ~ nurturing, protective, time for quiet inner reflection
- **Buffalo** ~ message from ancestors, strength, Great Spirit message as well, sacrifice for the greater good
- **Otter** ~ time for fun and play, let your hair down
- **Whale** ~ time for music, work with sound therapy
- **Lion** ~ courage, strength, a time of confidence
- **Lynx** ~ strong intuitive time, seeing beyond the veil
- **Snake** ~ time of change, shedding the skin of the old, kundalini energy, also beware of the sneaky influences around you
- **Butterflies** ~ transformation, a beautiful one at that, a shift inside and out
- **Fox** ~ a sneaky person is around, beware, the trickster
- **Lizards** ~ pay attention to your dreamtime
- **Ant** ~ time to connect with community, like-minded people
- **Dolphin** ~ playfulness, higher intelligence, get in touch with your emotions

There are many, many more animals that could be listed here! I encourage you to investigate further with books, the Internet, meditation and through your dreams as well.

Animal Communication

The area of animal communication is one where some people connect easily and naturally with animals. Some do not, and whatever is going on with their pet is a mystery.

I am often asked how we can communicate psychically with animals or even talk with them telepathically. Well, the answer is pretty simple. Work on your intuition, and you will become more psychically aware. It does not matter if you are trying to connect with a human, plant, or animal. Energy is energy; psychic ability is still psychic ability. You are intending to connect with soul energy.

Animals do communicate more in pictures than words. If you send an image or movie to their third eye, you may start receiving messages via pictures from them. A good practice would be sending from your third eye to theirs the movie or vision of them walking to you. Eventually they will come to you without speaking a word.

Often, I get questions about animals who are not feeling well. I have a few suggestions to see what may be going on. These methods are not in place of traditional medicine and treatment! While the animal is still, take your left hand and scan over the body from the top to the bottom. Take note if an area feels heavy or stagnant. If you should feel a denser energy with the pet, run chi, or light, or energy through the palm of your hand. You might notice they start to relax a little bit more. The problem could simply be they ate something they shouldn't have or are having a problem with gas, etc.

You may also grab your pendulum and use the pendulum instead of your hand for healing and detection. The pendulum could move counterclockwise, slowly, wobbly or not at all. If it moves any of these ways there is possibly a problem in that area. You may hold the pendulum over

Psychic Development 101

the area until it is clear or run energy through your hands.

You might receive pictures or images as to what is going on. Remember this is not in place of medical care of your animal! Be smart. If there isn't an improvement, then take the animal to your vet.

You can most certainly practice reading for other people's animals by looking at pictures as well. The animal does not need to be in the room. I will say again that energy is energy. By looking into the eyes of a living being, you are able to connect soul to soul. By listening to the messages of the soul, you are able to hear and receive messages. I have used this method for myself and during psychic development classes with success.

Animals are an excellent gauge of the character of people. If your pet does not like someone, I would be on guard. They are able to read people because they can sense lower vibrational energies as well as intentions. They use their primal skills.

Animals can also sense when spirits are present either in the home or on the property. An indicator can be they are barking and licking the air at "nothing" as well as making whimpering noises because they are trying to let you know someone is around. Also, pay attention to the hair on the back of the neck of your pet. The hair standing up is a sign of possible, impending danger.

I guarantee that by becoming more observant of the animal kingdom, you are receiving a cosmic heads up or two. Who couldn't use a little more guidance? Why not work hand in hand with all living creatures? This is why the creator put us here - to live in harmony with all living things.

4 Card Animal Spread

You can use any deck of animal cards. I recommend *Medicine Wheel Cards* by Jamie Sams as well as Steven Farmer's *Animal Spirit Guides*. There are many, many animal oracle/tarot cards.

You will pull 4 cards after asking the question, "Where am I right now in my life?"

Card 1 - place in the direction of the East

Card 2 - place in the direction of the South

Card 3 - place in the direction of the West

Card 4 - place in the direction of the North

What Does Each Direction Mean?

East - thoughts, where you are with your mind, ideas

South - the course of action needed, also the type of healing needed

West - inner reflection, where you are emotionally, your desires

North - what you are manifesting, also guidance from your ancestors

This is a nice spread to use maybe once a month.

FINAL THOUGHTS

By now I am sure you have been noticing that your intuition is becoming more spot on, you are able to clear your energy fields, you know how to sage, and when you select your crystals, you have become a master at cleansing and clearing them.

What I love most about the metaphysical field is there is always more to learn; the subjects and potential for self-exploration and growth are limitless.

I hope you have enjoyed this compilation of my years of self-study and practical application of the material.

From My Heart to Yours, Namaste'

Laurie

ABOUT THE AUTHOR

Laurie is originally from Queens/New Hyde Park in New York. Yes, she is a Long Island Medium. Laurie relocated to Ft. Myers, Florida, in 1990, and Ft. Myers has been her home ever since. She and Jim, her husband, have been together since 1987, and they have two teenage children, Jimmy and Nicole. Laurie is eternally grateful for the support and love her family provides her.

Laurie Barraco is the Owner of The Mystical Moon, a metaphysical center in Ft. Myers, Florida. www.themysticalmoon.com

ABOUT THE ARTIST

Jodi Lynn LaMure

www.listeningheartart.com

Laurie Recommends:

www.Lauriebarraco.com

www.Themysticalmoon.com

www.TMMinabox.com

www.Mindtripproductions.com

21 Days to Transformation

This 21 day program with tracks for AM and PM has been created to help you transform yourself with the power of vibration and thought.

Healing With Liquid Light

Journey to a place of deep relaxation and Crystal bowl healing, with this guided meditation. Listen to the beautiful Crystal Bowls and Ocean sounds, whil you follow a guided meditation designed to bring you to a place of deep healing.

For ordering, call 239-939-3339

Or visit www.themysticalmoon.com

Psychic Development 101

Made in the USA
Charleston, SC
19 July 2014